History of Korea

A Captivating Guide to Korean History, Including Events Such as the Mongol Invasions, the Split into North and South, and the Korean War

Free Bonus from Captivating History (Available for a Limited time)

Hi History Lovers!

Now you have a chance to join our exclusive history list so you can get your first history ebook for free as well as discounts and a potential to get more history books for free! Simply visit the link below to join.

Captivatinghistory.com/ebook

Also, make sure to follow us on Facebook, Twitter and Youtube by searching for Captivating History.

Contents

Introduction

The Korean Peninsula today is divided into two, but there was a time when this peninsula was divided into many states. Over the course of time, and besieged by expansive transient dynasties outside of this modest piece of land, many clans and tribes overran its regions. Of all those malicious and greedy potential overlords, none managed to prevail. The soil is rich with the blood of the people who made Korea happen, and it is the Korean people who rose victorious among the maelstrom of dead empires led by hated tyrants and wars fought by people in lands far beyond their own. The Koreans are survivors, known for their persistence and courage.

As Korea had long been seen as a gateway to other countries and the Yellow Sea, it was harassed for years by larger countries who were either on their way to somewhere else, like China, or who wanted a springboard to control the trade and colonization of the archipelagoes, smaller countries, and islands around the Pacific Ocean. The Western countries had interests in Korea, too, in order to curtail the full control of the Pacific to only one country, as well as to open Korea up to trade. As a result of these competing forces, Korea isolated itself during the latter half of the 19th century. In 1910, Japan annexed Korea and ruled it with an iron fist, even to the point of assimilating the unique culture of Korea into its own culture. In other words, they wanted to make it "disappear." The Koreans, however, fought long and hard to preserve their individuality as a nation. They eschewed control by other forces, even friendly ones, in order to preserve their unique cultural and political identity.

Even though Korea fought long and hard to remain one individual nation, they were eventually split into two. Western nations have made some overtures toward helping them achieve that unification and see an end to the Korean conflict. However, today, both North and South Korea want to lead that effort and do it their own way. Although Korea was granted its independence after two wars, the Korean people have it in their blood to be one undivided country, and they plan to work laboriously until that can be achieved in a way that is acceptable to both sides.

Chapter 1 – Land of the Bear

The Devil's Gate

In the cold dark cave of Chertovy Vorota, also known as the Devil's Gate, in northeastern Russia, lay her skull, long since abandoned by the ravages of Neolithic times from around 5700 BCE. No one knows her name, but she has achieved fame since she left geneticists with a record of the racial and ethnic origin of the hardy Korean people. The first people there fished in the frigid waters of the northern Pacific for salmon, cod, and hake. In addition, they hunted elk and moose. Unlike other primitive people, they were lactose intolerant, so they didn't milk any of the animals they hunted. Genome researchers also indicate that they raised agricultural products like rice and wheat to offset their high-protein diets. This was due to an influx of Neolithic people from southeastern Asia, where the growing season was longer. Later migrations show that the Han Chinese people from west of the Yellow River emigrated to the region, but there is plentiful evidence that many Chinese came to Korea much earlier (around 9,000 years ago). The Han Chinese were one of the largest ethnic groups in ancient China. They also brought the delightful mandarin orange plants with them for propagating.

With the arrival of the agricultural people came the development of the "paddy-field," which was a step-wise segmented area flooded with water to foster the growth of rice.

Early people settling there lived in pit-houses consisting of a mud and straw roof over a dug-out pit. Or, as in the case of the woman from Chertovy Vorota, they lived in caves. They cooked their rice and grains in cups and bowls made of clay decorated with "comb-patterns." This type of pottery originated during the Mumun period, which lasted from 1500 to 300 BCE. Korea is actually the only place in the world where this unique style can be found.

Shellfish was originally plentiful along the coasts, but archeologists are quick to point out the fact that the supply of shellfish diminished because of overexploitation and population growth. They theorized this happened during the Late Mumun period (550 to 300 BCE).

The lack of shellfish resulted in the growth of farming activity. Farming was mainly conducted in southern Korea, while those who lived in the northern area of the peninsula favored meat and fish. To eat their food, as well as to make weapons, Koreans fashioned axes, knives, and cooking utensils out of bronze, which is made from heating copper and tin. These molten metals were then poured into clay molds.

Songguk-ri

Songguk-ri is an archeological site that contains only whispers about the civilization that lived in the central-western region of South Korea in the Middle and Late Mumun period (c. 850 to 300 BCE). Because of the arrangement of the pit-houses and the existence of large walls at Songguk-ri, it has been concluded that there were divisions among the tribes that lived there. Greenstones (primarily jade) and intricately designed bronze daggers found at burial sites seem to indicate that there were chiefs, who, along with their families, would have lorded over the rest of the common population.

The existence of the Songguk-ri wall indicates that there were competition and conflict between the various clans. In addition, there was a stratified social structure. As discussed earlier, the Chinese migrated to Korea. Between 475 to 221 BCE, the states of China were at war until the Qin Dynasty took over. Although most of the Korean migrants were from the state of Han, some were not. Those people brought their hostilities with them to Korea, and some of the settlements were burned and subsequently abandoned.

Within the individual clan societies, there is evidence that shows that the elites in the population controlled their subjects through the distribution of arable lands and labor demands. Most likely, the elite people had the subservient classes supply food for them, and they received more than enough to sustain themselves. Indications are that the food for the noble classes and royalty was of a higher quality. Researchers have found the remains of rice cakes and rice wine (*cheongju*), which would have been considered gourmet food. Because it was primarily an agrarian economy, control of the economy equaled control of the people, and so, the leaders provided incentives for food producers who had larger crop yields.

The other caste that emerged during this period was the one devoted to craft production. Besides household objects and weapons, Koreans produced beads made out of jade. These beads were often used as a sort of currency. Everyone had to pay tribute to the central leadership, and they used beads or barter to do so. The artifacts found of these crafts include mirrors, jewelry, and an assortment of weapons.

Later on, Korean craftsmen manufactured specialized swords. The most notable sword that has been discovered is the "Liaoning sword," or the seven-branched sword. Artifacts indicate that this type of sword originated in the northern peninsula and then became popular in other regions. Archeologists debate about whether or not it was used as a weapon, although the inscriptions on it would seem to indicate so. The characters are inlaid with gold, and on one side of the sword, it reads in part: "Using the sword repels 100 enemy soldiers. It is bestowed to the duke lord."

They Had Heat!

Korean winters are long and cold, especially in the north. To heat their houses, a fire would be built alongside the home in a pit, allowing heat to flow into a short basement under the floorboards. Rocks were fastened to the underside of the floor to help retain heat. There was an outlet on the opposite side of the house for a stove and, beyond that, a flue with a free-standing chimney that funneled the smoke out. The heating system was called *ondol*, and it would be built when the house was erected.

Since the fire was extinguished at night as a safety measure, the houses cooled and were very cold by late morning. Of course, they were relit, but it took a long time for the air in the rooms to heat back up. The room closest to the fire pit was very hot, while the room farthest away was much cooler. Even so, this heating system was incredibly sophisticated for a primitive culture.

Creation Myth

Ancient historians in 7th-century China wrote that a god by the name of Hwanung craved to live in the valleys and mountains of earth. He was the son of the "Lord of Heaven," Hwanin. Hwanung was granted the assistance of the spirits of the Rain, Wind, and Clouds in his quest to find land on earth, and he descended on Paektu Mountain with his followers. According to the legend, a tiger and a bear befriended him. The two animals prayed to become human, so Hwanung placed them into a solitary cave. Whoever would persist without food or water the longest would be the winner. In time, the tiger tired, gave in to his baser instincts, and left the cave to hunt. However, the bear persisted and did become human. She was named Ungnyeo, and Hwanung fell in love with her. They wed and gave birth to a son named Dangun Wanggeom. Dangun settled in the northern area of Korea with 3,000 followers and established the settlement of Gojoseon.

The Three Kingdoms: Goguryeo

By 18 BCE, Korea had been split into three prominent kingdoms: Goguryeo in the northern and central parts of the peninsula and Baekje and Silla on the southern tip.

Around 37 BCE, Goguryeo was first called "Gojoseon." They engaged in trade with the Han Chinese throughout the Bronze Age. Because of their language similarity with the native Japanese (Japonic language), they traded with Japan and even accepted some of them into their population.

In time, Gojoseon collapsed under a succession of rather weak descendants of Dangun. Under his descendant, King Dongmyeongseong, or "Jumong," the region was renamed Goguryeo (also spelled as Koguryo), and it became more powerful and larger after battles with the Chinese and nomadic tribes from Manchuria, Mongolia, and part of Russia. Jumong was a militaristic autocrat, and his successors followed in his footsteps. By 242 CE, Goguryeo had expanded north and doubled in size.

The use of iron for weaponry greatly assisted the monarchs of Goguryeo in conquering territory from China. Iron was plentiful in the rocks of Goguryeo. It could be melted down, but it could not be poured in molds like bronze. Instead, it had to be hammered into shape by a metalworker while still hot. Iron became more desirable as it was much stronger than bronze, which tended to bend or break.

The Three Kingdoms: Baekje

Baekje was the second of the three stable kingdoms. Legends tell a story about the son of King Jumong, Yuri, who was a troublemaker with poor manners. Yuri ran away from home when his father was away warring with the princes of the kingdom. When Jumong returned, he was furious. In order for his son and heir to be redeemed, Jumong buried half a sword and challenged Yuri to find the other half. It was Jumong's objective that Yuri learn how to start and finish a difficult task. When Yuri found the other half of the sword, he was reunited with his father.

After Jumong's wife died, Jumong took on a new wife named Soseono, and they had two sons—Onjo and Biryu. The two of them were always obedient and loyal. Since they would have no inheritance after their father died due to Yuri making up with his father, Jumong had them go southward and create their own state. The two brothers quarreled, as brothers often do, and each set up their own state in the southern part of Goguryeo.

Unfortunately, Biryu's segment, called Sipje, was totally unsuitable for productive habitation, as it was full of salt marshes. Humbly, he moved to his brother's neighboring state, Baekje, to the west. It lies beneath the shadow of the great Bukhan Mountain, which can be seen behind the current-day city of Seoul. Biryu couldn't handle this deep failure of his and committed suicide. However, his generous brother, Onjo, welcomed all of Biryu's relatives and subjects into his kingdom.

Onjo needed to expand his state to integrate all these new subjects, so he had to fight with elements from the Samhan confederacy farther south in order to create a larger state. The largest of these city-states was ruled by the kings of the Mahan confederacy, which was a part of the greater Samhan confederacy. When one of the Mahan kings committed suicide because he couldn't defend his territory against the forces of Onjo, he asked that Onjo treat his people with mercy. Onjo did so, and he gradually absorbed the Mahan region of the Samhan confederacy into the Baekje Kingdom.

While he was running the state of Baekje, Onjo's warriors had to continually defend the lands from nomadic peoples called the Malgal, or Mohe, a Tungusic people. They were originally from the southern districts of Manchuria and often pillaged Baekje around 5 BCE because it had become quite prosperous. Onjo proved to be successful in defending his lands, leading to a long line of rulers.

The Three Kingdoms: Silla

In 57 BCE, an ancient legend relates that a great light shone into a dark forest like a spotlight. A great "chicken dragon" pranced into the heavenly light and laid a large white egg. From that egg, a human baby hatched. His name was Park (also known as Bak or Pak) Hyeokgeose, and he founded the magnificent state of Silla to the east of Baekje.

The hills and mountains of Silla yielded much gold, and the area became a haven for craftsmen. Silla is known today for its intricate golden jewelry. The royal women of this state wore beautiful golden earrings, while the males owned golden ceremonial daggers in scabbards studded with jade and turquoise. The crowns were likewise delicate, consisting of a band of gold with two golden antler spikes and dangling golden beads.

Park Hyeokgeose wore such a crown until 4 CE, which was when his son took up the mantle. In time, a hereditary monarchy was established, and the state operated like a feudal society. It was a land of peace until there was friction between Silla and Baekje over territorial boundaries. Silla allied itself with Goguryeo for protection. In time, though, Goguryeo expanded southward and established a capital at Pyongyang. In 427 CE, Goguryeo started expanding even farther south. Due to the work of King Nulji of Silla, Silla and Baekje were able to resolve their differences, and the two states united their armed forces against Goguryeo. They drove the Goguryeo people farther north toward the Han River in the locale of South Korea's modern-day capital city of Seoul.

Silla, like the other Korean kingdoms, had a hereditary line of rulers. The system of inheritance of the throne was based on the bone-rank system, which was a caste system that segregated the levels of society. "Sacred bone" was the top rank, meaning that the ruler had royal blood from both their father and mother. The oldest surviving piece of the written history of Korea is the *Samguk Sagi* (or, in English, *History of the Three Kingdoms*), which was written in 1145 and is used today as a reference for archeologists and historians. According to the *Samguk Sagi,* Sol Kyedu, the son of an official, said: "In Silla, bone rank is the key to employment."

This system applied to women as well. Although it wasn't incredibly common for women to have power in Silla, it did happen on occasion, and the idea of "sacred bone" helped to work in their favor. In 632, there were no male descendants, so Seondeok ruled Silla after proving herself to her father, becoming the first queen of Silla. Initially, she was ridiculed by the nobles, and Emperor Taizong of the Tang Dynasty of China asked, "If you do not have an appropriate leader, shall I send you a king?" In time, though, the Korean people came to love her. She was concerned about the welfare of her people, and at the beginning of her reign, she sent out inspectors so she could be informed about the needs of her people, specifically the elderly, the poor, and the abandoned.

In the 1280s, another ancient historical tome was written called the *Samguk Yusa* (or, in English, *Memorabilia of the Three Kingdoms*). As opposed to the *Samguk Sagi*, the *Samguk Yusa* was a record of the legends and beliefs of the early societies of Korea. According to the *Samguk Yusa*, Seondeok had clairvoyant abilities. It stated that she saw white frogs croaking by the Jade Gate pond in the winter in a vision. Since frogs croak angrily like soldiers in a battle, Seondeok interpreted this vision as a sign that a great battle would occur between Silla and the people from the west (Baekje) and that Silla would prevail in the end. Queen Seondeok told her generals to search out enemy infiltrators who would be found hiding in the forests near Silla, preparing to attack. It happened just as she had said, and Silla engaged in war with the Baekje Kingdom. Having caught the Baekje warriors by surprise, the army of Silla slaughtered over one thousand soldiers.

After Seondeok's successor, Queen Jindeok took the throne, she wanted to court the favor of the Tang Dynasty in China. She sent a complimentary poem to Emperor Gaozong, which said, in part, "Great Tang created the celestial empire…He rules over the whole creation and gives luster to everything—his deep benevolence is matched only by the sun and the moon." Gaozong was highly flattered by the beautiful poem, and so, the Tang Dynasty of China was favorably disposed toward Silla.

After Jindeok died in 654, Muyeol rose to the throne. King Muyeol was an accomplished strategist, and he made a military alliance with the Tang Dynasty of China. In 660, both conquered Baekje, leaving only Goguryeo to contend with.

Munmu, the next king who took over in 661, established an educational system to instruct all of his officials. They were also exposed to the Chinese classics. Munmu is also remembered for his military accomplishments. In 668, Munmu managed to defeat Goguryeo, meaning that Munmu was the first ruler to see the Korean Peninsula unified, which led to the Unified Silla period, also known as Later Silla. Munmu also had to deal with the Tang Dynasty during his rule. In 674, the mighty army of the Tang attempted to absorb Silla. However, they were defeated two years later in 676.

Silla, by this point, had become a great sea power, as it had a generous coastline along the Pacific Ocean. It conducted trade with local countries, including Japan. However, Japan became a threat to Korea during this period. They had a steady stream of pirates that attacked the port cities, and some of the Japanese forces raided the towns in Silla. Munmu set up defenses along its eastern coast, which did help to repel the invaders. As he aged, he asked that he might be entombed underwater. Korean beliefs in the 7th century indicate that he thought he could then become the "Dragon of the East Sea" by doing this and continue to protect his people. Today, one can see an impressive rocky island under which the body of the beloved king was interred.

Chapter 2 – The Dragon of the East Sea

The Great Ch'oyong

The *Samguk Yusa,* or *Memorabilia of the Three Kingdoms*, told a story about the Dragon of the East Sea. The people of Silla revered the royal family, especially King Munmu, and told stories of his accomplishments along with personal tales about his trials and tribulations. His story, as well as other stories, are peppered throughout this ancient text. Here is another one of the tales, which relates a story about the Dragon of the East Sea.

In the 9th century, the king of Silla, Heongang, failed to make his offerings to the great Dragon of the East Sea. Clouds shrouded the land and sea. Heongang was a humble king, and so, he asked his subjects why the great dragon frowned upon him. They told him he hadn't made his offerings and was negligent in his meditations. After making the expected offerings, the Dragon of the East Sea appeared before the king and his seven sons. There was a great celebration among the people, filled with music and dancing. After this tale, the *Samguk Yusa* goes on to tell of the misfortune of one of his sons, Ch'oyong.

Ch'oyong came home after the celebration to find that an evil spirit had possessed his wife and lured another man into their marriage bed. As related in the *Samguk Yusa*, Ch'oyong said, "Having caroused far into the night in the moonlit capital, I return home and in my bed, Behold, four legs. Two were mine; Whose are the other two? Formerly two were mine; What shall be done now they are taken?" Ch'oyong was heartbroken by this, but he spared the two and withdrew in silent resignation. After that virtuous act, the evil spirit appeared before him and said that he was impressed with Ch'oyong's response, which was not one of rage. The evil spirit then promised that whenever Ch'oyong's likeness is displayed, the evil spirit will not return.

Korean Buddhism

Back in the 4th century, Buddhism was introduced to Korea. It originated from India and was transported to China and then Korea. Buddhists believe in four truths: 1) existence brings suffering; 2) the cause of suffering is craving; 3) there is a way to end suffering; and 4) one needs to break one's earthly attachments. That will lead to the state of nirvana, or perfect happiness. The means by which one attains nirvana is to follow an eightfold path consisting of right understanding, right thought, right speech, right action, right livelihood, right effort, right mindfulness, and right concentration. Koreans added one more step to this path: the requirement to settle all disputes peaceably. The last step reflects the lessons derived from the historical struggle of the three kingdoms to unite.

Korean Confucianism

During the 4th century, Confucian beliefs were carried into Korea through the Han Chinese. Most of them were then living in the areas north of the Korean Peninsula. Confucianism is a humanistic belief system. It didn't conflict with other religions but was rather a structure for understanding how to live in a society with each other peacefully. It focuses on *ren*, which means that one learns how to live life in such a way as to promote order, peace, love for fellow humans, ethics, and respect for parents within society. Benevolence and compassion are virtues that flow from this paradigm and bring about wisdom. Its founder, Confucius, supported obedience to rightful authority figures and the observance of sacred rituals. He once said, "To master oneself and return to ritual propriety is human-heartedness."

Ancestor worship is derived from these beliefs, but it isn't "worship" per se; it is more a recognition of the contribution from prior generations that has formed a lasting imprint in the minds and hearts of the living. There were specific rituals created within extended families for memorializing the lives of the ancestors. Many are still practiced today and are not seen as a contradiction to other faiths, even Christianity.

The Golden Age

Korea, now united in 676, produced many great masterpieces of art and architecture. Many of these sites are still present today and manifest the distinctive beauty of Korea during the 7th and 8th centuries.

The Ansi fortress is an example of how architecture and the outcome of battles are related. Goguryeo in northern Korea had as many as 2,400 fortresses. Korean fortresses were built very differently than Chinese fortresses. Koreans used stones that were carefully shaped into oblong blocks; they were mostly made of granite quarried in the mountains, and these blocks were slotted together very carefully. The Chinese, on the other hand, used earthen-style fortresses, which were built of bricks, although sometimes they utilized mounds of earth. In 645, when Goguryeo battled with the Tang Dynasty of China in the Siege of Ansi, the Chinese built a giant earth mound from which to launch an attack. Because it was only made of earth, it collapsed. Thus, Korea prevailed against the Tang.

The Seokguram Grotto is another interesting piece of architecture. It was built in 774 and still contains a great statue of Buddha that looks out to the sea. The position of the Buddha relates to the history of

Korea since recurring threats to their land came from Japan and other seafaring peoples. The great Buddha statue shows Buddha with his right hand in the *dhyana mudra* position, indicating that the flow of energy from within is one of concentration. His left hand is in the *bhumisparsha mudra* position, symbolizing the earth. Thus, Buddha touches the spirit of life and shows unity, which is reminiscent of the Korean struggle to remain united. There is a central rotunda within the grotto with carefully carved sculptures of devas (angels), bodhisattvas (students), and disciples of the great Buddha. It is made of granite quarried in the eastern mountains.

The grotto is combined with the Bulguksa temple complex, which is made of gleaming white granite. There are three terraces with pillared railings of wood, and three pagodas are perched on top. The Bulguksa temple complex, rebuilt in 774, teaches through its architecture the journey of a Buddhist reaching nirvana. For example, within the temple, there are two halls, one of which is called the "Hall of No Words." This means that belief cannot be taught by mere words alone. This temple has undergone many embellishments throughout the years and is considered the foremost Buddhist temple in South Korea.

Two pagodas at the Gameunsa Temple Site, located on the eastern coast of Korea, were built in the 7th century to celebrate the victory of King Munmu over the Tang Chinese and the Japanese pirates. They were built from multiple oblong granite stones, and the stone structures have a three-tiered roof system. Originally, the pagodas were used for sacrificial rites. The Gameunsa pagodas survived the ravages of time and are featured today in many of the tourist brochures for Korea.

Pottery flourished during the Korean golden age as well. Pots and vessels from this period display natural themes, such as leaves or flowers. It is a simplistic, free-flowing, and open design, neither complex nor pattern-adherent. Potters painted each of their pieces individually, and they often used one or two colors. Pigments were made from the minerals found in the mountains.

Not all of the art had religious themes. In the fine tombs of the Korean nobles and kings, there are giant murals depicting the activities of daily life that feature the deceased couple. Other themes painted on the walls of the tombs show the occupations of the common people, like hunting, fishing, and farming. There are frescoes in these tombs that use exquisite decorative techniques to paint lotus flowers, fish, horses, tigers, deer, and dragons. Korean art shows a Chinese influence, but the themes draw it closer to the history of Korea because they use fewer pictographs.

Due to Chinese influences, woodblock printing was created during this time. Craftsmen carved characters in raised relief on blocks of wood, and ink was applied to the raised portions. The characters were to be read from right to left, like in a mirror image. The subject matters initially were about Buddhist *sutras*, or sayings. The Great Dharani Sutra is the earliest example of Korean woodblocks and was found inside the Bulguksa temple complex in South Korea. It is considered to be the oldest printed text in the world.

Balhae

To escape the earlier battles of the three kingdoms in Korea, many people fled to the north and settled there. They were ethnically related to the Manchurian and eastern Russian people. They despised the Tang rule and united with the nomadic Mohe people to free themselves from the government of Korea, which was heavily influenced by the Tang culture.

Dae Jo-yeong, a general from Goguryeo, had orders from the last king of Goguryeo to establish a new kingdom, and he chose the territory northeast of Korea to establish his new state. He and his Mohe allies had to defeat the Chinese who were occupying that region first. In 698, he and his army defeated the Tang Chinese at the Battle of Tianmenling. They called their new land Balhae, which is also referred to as Parhae in some academic sources.

In 732, the second king of Balhae, Mu, expanded the territory of Balhae even more. Once it was fully settled, Balhae opened up relations with Japan, an association which they nurtured for years. In addition to the officials of Balhae, poets, like Chongso and Injong, served as foreign diplomats. Balhae fostered the arts, and although only a few artifacts remain from that period, they are stately and imposing. The area is known for its two huge stone lanterns erected on huge pillars.

The last king of Balhae, Seon, greatly expanded Balhae and conquered some lands in today's North Korea. Balhae also encompassed portions of today's northeast China and Russia. Balhae was so strong at this point that Silla had to build a wall in 821 to prevent Balhae from encroaching on their territory.

However, there are no surviving records of Balhae after King Seon ended his reign in 830, so it is not known what happened next. His grandson did take the throne, but scholars don't have much information on him. What is known definitively is that the Khitans took over Balhae in 926. The Khitans were not a new problem; they had harassed Balhae throughout the years. Historians debate over their origin. Some conjecture that they came from Manchuria and Mongolia, while others contend that they originated from the Eurasian steppes. They were expert horsemen, wore furs, and were very skilled with the bow and arrow. They raised cattle and were meat-eaters, which horrified the vegetarian Buddhists, who called them "barbarians." The Khitans had formed the Liao Dynasty in 916 and were headquartered in China near the Yalu River, which borders North Korea.

Although Balhae did receive some aid from Goguryeo in the south, their culture and society were destroyed by the Khitans. Many of the people of Balhae migrated to Goguryeo, which protected them, and they were referred to as a "married country," meaning that the people of Goguryeo felt a kinship with them. Those who stayed in Balhae found themselves being ruled by the Khitans of the Dongdan Kingdom, which was later annexed by the Liao Dynasty in 936.

In 946, Paektu Mountain, a volcano, burst open, propelling a Plinian (hot gaseous) blast that sent steaming smoke and debris as far as the stratosphere. Following that was the pyroclastic (rock-spewing) explosion, which sent tremendous rocks and ash into the region. This eruption is one of the most powerful in history. Following that, the ancient records fall silent. Historians, therefore, conclude that this tremendous natural disaster wiped out most of the lands once known as Balhae.

The Later Three Kingdoms

Between 892 and 935, Later Silla started to disintegrate. Under the administration of Queen Jinseong (ruled 887 to 897), corruption had started to seep into the government. Taxes rose to supplement the money that officials were embezzling from the treasury, and because of the heavy tax burden, famines occurred. Simultaneously, political rivalries also arose within the administration. Revolts and decentralization took place as the regional people outside of the capital of Later Silla, Gyeongju, banded together to survive.

Taking advantage of the strife in the kingdom, some rebels sought to revive the kingdoms of Baekje and Goguryeo. The cultural differences between the three states also gave impetus to this separation. Goguryeo was allied with the Tang Chinese and showed the influences of that culture. Baekje resurrected itself and was primarily a trading region, but Silla was wrought with internal strife among the nobles and kings clamoring for power.

Later Baekje

The kingdom of Silla gave rise to powerful generals, one of whom was Gyeon Hwon. In 892, the peasants had been severely downtrodden and burdened with heavy taxation. Taking advantage of their dissatisfaction, Gyeon united them and formed a mighty army in order to overthrow the rulers and nobles. After conquering the large city districts of Wansanju and Mujinju, he declared himself king, and the area was then called Hubaekje ("Later Baekje).

In 927, Gyeon Hwon attacked the kingdom of Silla. He and his forces handily won, and the king of Silla, Gyeongae, chose to commit suicide over placing his fate in the hands of Gyeon Hwon. After that, Gyeon Hwon established a puppet monarch on the throne before turning his attention to Goryeo (which had previously been Later Goguryeo; see below). He led a full-scale attack there in the present-day city of Andong, located in the mid-eastern portion of Korea, but he lost. He continued to attempt to gain control, and sporadic battles ensued between Later Baekje and Goryeo.

While this was going on, internal strife was tearing the kingdom apart. Gyeon Hwon was deposed by his son, Gyeon Singeom, with the aid of some of his other brothers after Singeom had been passed over as heir to the throne. Gyeon Hwon fled to Goryeo, who welcomed his military experience with open arms.

Once Silla surrendered to Goryeo in 935, Gyeon Hwon was allowed to go after Later Baekje that same year. In doing so, he brought about the downfall of the very kingdom he founded.

Later Goguryeo

Like Gyeon Hwon of Baekje, Gung Ye, a one-eyed monk, was initially a Silla military prince. In 891, he united with the rebel factions and quickly rose in power. He was known as being a cruel and rigid leader. He was extremely self-centered and began referring to himself as the reincarnation of the Maitreya Buddha later on life; the Maitreya Buddha occupies the most prestigious place in Buddhism, even today. During the course of his life, he executed his own wife and two of his sons, whom he saw as rivals. When some of his fellow monks admonished him, he executed them as well. Gung Ye, who had a very changeable nature, joined with other warlords as time went on before amassing enough power to stage his own rebellion. In 901, he turned on the other warlords and proclaimed himself king of Hugoguryeo (known as Later Goguryeo). Due to his erratic nature, the name of the country was later changed to Majin, and the capital was moved to Cheorwon, a fortress located in a mountainous region.

In 911, the name of the country was changed yet again, this time to Taebong. Gung Ye appointed a prime minister named Wang Geon, also known as Taejo of Goryeo, two years later. Some of the nobles from the ruling families conspired with Wang Geon to stage a coup. While many historians indicate they did this because of objections to Gung Ye's tyrannical rule, they themselves were just as warlike when given authority. Wang Geon and the nobles usurped the throne from Gung Ye in 918, and he was killed by either one of his own soldiers or by peasants after having escaped the palace. Wang Geon was placed on the throne, and he renamed the kingdom as Goryeo, also spelled as Koryo, which is where the name Korea is derived from.

Later Silla

At the beginning of the 9th century, the nobles had grabbed a huge power base in Silla. The people were very unhappy over the tax burden and the constant conflicts that erupted in the different regions of Silla. There were famines caused by the high taxes the nobles collected, and there was no system for supplying the people with food and grain when their crops failed. As the nobles were warring with each other, the whole state of Silla was starting to disintegrate. As a result, Silla was losing many of their people since they moved to other parts of Korea, China, and even Japan.

A young man by the name of Jang Bogo arose from the population. He had integrity and mustered the favor of the Korean people. When Jang was studying his martial arts skills in China, the people from Silla who had fled from there were being poorly treated by the Chinese. Some of their women were abducted and sold into slavery, pirates raided their ships, and bandits roamed around the towns. When the Silla people met Jang Bogo, they were impressed with his chivalry and forthrightness. They even asked him to lead and defend them, which he did so in 825. He established a small private fleet, and in 827, he presented a petition to the king of Silla, Heungdeok, to construct a fortress along the coast to protect the fishermen. Due to his skills, a thriving maritime industry grew on the Yellow Sea. His fleet increased substantially, and the fishermen and merchants from Silla were conducting business not only with the legitimate Tang traders but with Persians and Arabians as well. Jang was a masterful negotiator, and his ships exploited what is called the "Maritime Silk Road," which ran down the coast of Korea and the coast of southern China, down along Vietnam, and around India, among other routes. Trade in aromatics and spices thrived during this era as a result.

In Silla proper, however, there were vicious succession battles. The reigns of the kings from 828 to 927 were very short-lived, as each made war on their predecessors. The territory was also frequently attacked by other forces, most notably those of Gyeon Hwon of Later Baekje and Taejo of Goryeo. Severely weakened by the wars, the last king of Silla, Gyeongsun, abdicated and surrendered the throne to Wang Geon, with Later Baekje soon following suit.

Thus, the three kingdoms were again reunited in 935. The greatest advantage of this reunification was the fact that the three cultural elements melded together and created the basis for the country of Korea.

Chapter 3 – Dynasties Rise and Fall

The Goryeo Dynasty

Once the Later Three Kingdoms all came under the control of Wang Geon, he established what is known as the Goryeo Dynasty. The power of the noble families had been a perennial problem on the peninsula. Wang Geon was a man of peace who looked toward unity in order to create an orderly society, making the country a fertile land for the arts and Buddhism. Cleverly, he married women from all the noble families and had 25 sons and 9 daughters by them. Wang Geon established a hierarchical system of administrators and passed reforms to strengthen monarchical authority. What's more, he freed prisoners of war from the tumultuous period of the conflicts among the old kingdoms. This was a strategic move, as it increased the tax base and helped to make the treasury healthy.

Wang Geon's third son, Jeongjong, formed a huge army of 300,000 men to defend the territory of Goryeo against the troublesome Khitans, whose empire was the most powerful at the time. Wang Geon's fourth son, Gwangjong, opened up relations with the massive Song Dynasty in China in 962 to aid him in keeping the nomadic Khitans out of Goryeo. Aside from that, Gwangjong continued making reforms and created a systematic bureaucracy by initiating civil service examinations to assure the country had capable and knowledgeable leadership with clearly defined job roles.

Seongjong, who inherited the throne in 981, focused upon education in Goryeo and founded the Gukjagam University in 992, which helped to promote Confucian philosophy. The university library was stocked with many Chinese classics, as well as texts on science and mathematics.

The Goryeo-Khitan War

During Seongjong's reign, the pesky Liao Empire reared its head again. In 993, they attacked the northwestern border of Goryeo. Seeing that his troops were heavily outnumbered, Seongjong asked to negotiate peace terms and sent his negotiator, Seo Hui, to meet with the Khitan commander, Xiao Sunning. Xiao then said to Seo, "I am a nobleman from a powerful country. You must bow down before coming into my tent." Seo objected, saying that such behavior wasn't appropriate for two envoys. Xiao was amazed by Seo's courage and suggested that the two sit down as equals and discuss terms.

Goryeo agreed to three terms in the treaty: 1) the cessation of relations with the Song Dynasty, 2) the payment of an annual tribute, and 3) the adoption of the Liao calendar. Goryeo abided by all but one of the terms in the agreement—the relationship with the Song Dynasty. This was a major problem for the Khitans, as the Liao Empire were enemies of the Song.

The treaty, signed in 993, lasted until 1009, which was when the Khitans again attacked Goryeo. The king of Goryeo at the time was King Mokjong. However, political intrigue in Goryeo polluted the leadership, allowing a coup to occur under General Gang Jo. He assassinated King Mokjong and established military rule in Goryeo. The devious Khitans attacked at this time, claiming that they were avenging the dead king but more likely hoping to gain something out of the internal turmoil. As a result of the conflict, the capital was destroyed. However, the Khitans couldn't obtain the desired foothold needed and were forced to retreat. Knowing that the Khitans would eventually strike again, King Hyeonjong, who had been placed on the throne by Gang Jo, attempted to enter peace negotiations with the Liao Empire. Since the Liao Empire demanded too much—they wanted key areas of the northern region in exchange for peace, which would have given them a foothold in Goryeo—hostilities reignited between the two powers. Successive attacks continued along the border regions in 1015, 1016, and 1017. Each time, the two sides withdrew and repaired their border fortifications. No resolution was reached, and so, the sporadic attacks continued.

In 1018, King Hyeonjong of Goryeo employed the military talents of General Gang Gam-chan, as well as that of the Mongols. Before the Khitan warriors had amassed at the border, he dammed the river up with cowhides near Heungwajin. The Khitans came storming through toward the river and the fortress located there. When they crossed the Yalu River, the Gang Gam-chan had his troops dismantle the dam, and thousands of Khitans were drowned.

Once the Khitans reorganized, they marched toward the capital of Goryeo. However, the Goryeo warriors put up a fierce fight, and they forced the Khitans back north. Gang Gam-chan waited at the fortress in Gwiju for the Khitans. Not many details exist about this battle, but it is known that the Khitans were almost completely annihilated. After this battle, the Liao Empire and Goryeo enjoyed peace with each other until the Liao Empire fell in 1125.

The Thousand-li Wall

A *li* is a traditional unit of distance in China, and it has been used by other Asiatic peoples throughout the years. Its measurements have changed over time, but it measured about 323 meters (almost 1,060 feet) when the wall was built, and it measures around 500 meters (about 1,640 feet) today.

After the Goryeo-Khitan War, Goryeo erected this immense wall, which was built between 1033 and 1044. It connected the northern fortresses of Goryeo, and a portion of it remains today.

The Invasions of the Jurchen People

The Jurchens were a tribe of agrarian people who settled in the Siberian/Mongolian tundra. They were also referred to as the "reindeer people." However, during the 11th century, they were vassals of the Liao Empire. At that time, the Khitans of the Liao Dynasty had been attempting to move toward Goryeo in search of warmer lands. Their "slash-and-burn" technique of agricultural destruction stunted the growth of their grain crops, thus giving impetus to the need to relocate. The Jurchens lived in areas of the Chinese mainland as a minority, but in 1104, the Jurchens grew stronger and amassed in force around northern Goryeo. They often raided the lands of northern Goryeo during the time of the Goryeo-Khitan War.

Once the Goryeo-Khitan War was over, the experienced military general, Yun Gwan, approached King Sukjong of Goryeo to reorganize a segment of the army into cavalry and ground forces, which would become known as the Byeolmuban, to expel the Jurchens. In 1107, he invaded Jurchen territory to the north of Goryeo. Initially, he was repelled by the battle-hardened Jurchens, but he returned and successfully erected nine fortresses on the northern border. In 1108, the fortresses were abandoned in exchange for a non-aggression pact.

The Jurgens then turned their attention to the Khitan Liao Dynasty, as they wished to overthrow their status as vassals. In 1114, the Jurchens attacked and subdued them, after which they took over regions of northeastern China, which eventually culminated in the establishment of the Jin Dynasty in China. By 1125, the Jurchens had managed to subdue the Khitans, ending the Liao Dynasty.

However, from 1189 to 1234 (the year the Jin Dynasty ended), the Jurchens were involved in battles with the Mongols. In the beginning, the Jurchens of the Jin Dynasty constantly raided the property of the Mongols, who dwelled in the southern steppes. The Jin destroyed the rice paddies and the families who grew the rice. The Mongols responded in kind, and in 1211, the great Genghis Khan came raging through after having united many of the various nomadic tribes from Mongolia into a giant force of warriors. In 1234, their powerful leader, Ögedei Khan, the third son and chosen successor of Genghis Khan, put an end to the Jin Dynasty, repeating the words of his father, "The eternal sky has promised us victory and vengeance."

The Mongol Sweep

During Genghis Khan's lifetime, the relationship between Goryeo and the Mongols was a fairly peaceful one. Goryeo had actually aided the Mongols in some battles with the Chinese farther north, and the Mongols helped Goryeo subdue the Khitans when they attempted to invade Goryeo as they fled from the Mongol horde.

In 1225, though, this changed. The Mongol Empire began to demand tribute, and when the Mongol envoy was killed, the Mongols prepared for war. In 1231, Ögedei Khan, actually ordered an attack on Goryeo. The Mongols conquered the town of Anju, while the forces of Goryeo defended themselves at Kuju, cities that would be located in northern North Korea today. Goryeo had adopted the use of the siege tower from the ancient Romans, which consists of a wooden tower with stairways inside that helped an army mount a city wall. Between that and the use of flaming carts and arrows wetted by wads of burning human flesh, the Mongols were forced to withdraw from Kuju. General Saritai of the Mongol army rushed southwest in response. They were experts with the bow and arrow and were an extremely mobile force using hardy Asian Akhal-Teke horses that were used to the cold. The Mongols next captured the capital of Goryeo, Kaesong. The king of Goryeo, Gojong, realized that the Mongols were superb warriors and that they presented an enormous challenge to his forces, so he sued for peace. However, the tribute the Mongols demanded was ridiculously high, so Gojong urged his men to continue the fight. Despite his king's pleas, the military general of Goryeo, Choe U, decided to move the king and his family, as well as most of the population, to the island of Ganghwa, as he knew that the Mongols were superstitious about the sea.

Upset with this move by Goryeo, the Mongols launched another attack. Wave after wave of Mongol forces blasted their way south through Goryeo, and although the Mongols did try on several occasions to capture the well-fortified island, they were unable to do so. At the city of Cheoin, located near current-day Yongin in South Korea, the two sides clashed. General Saritai of the Mongols was slain by a participating monk, Kim Yun-hu. After the death of Saritai, the Mongol forces went into disarray and withdrew.

Although they hadn't captured all of the cities they laid their sights on, the Mongols destroyed crops and farmlands, employing scorched-earth tactics. This meant that not only were farmlands set afire, but any ancillary buildings, including barns, stables, and houses were destroyed. The farmers and their families were likewise killed if they resisted, as well as their animals.

In 1238, King Gojong, who was stationed on Ganghwa Island, agreed to the Mongols' demand that he send members of his royal family as hostages to their court. However, he didn't follow through, though. Instead, the king sent an unrelated family member. His ploy didn't work, and the Mongols insisted that the administration on Ganghwa Island move to the mainland, along with handing over members of the royal family as hostages. King Gojong again refused, sending distant family members to the Mongols. So, in 1247, the Mongols sent one of their most ferocious warlords, Amuqan, to Goryeo. He and his forces then pillaged and ravaged as much of the Korean Peninsula as possible. Some of the officials of Goryeo did move to the mainland, but the king still refused to give in to their demands.

In 1251, Möngke Khan became the head of the Mongol Empire. The stalemate over peace negotiations with Goryeo, however, continued. After much resistance and attacks by the Mongols, King Gojong finally gave in to the Mongols, moving his court back to the mainland. King Gojong then sent his stepson, Angyeong, as a hostage, and the Mongols agreed to a ceasefire in 1254. Soon, though, the Mongols found out there were still Goryeo officials on Ganghwa, and once Möngke Khan discovered that the teen boy wasn't a blood relative, there was no way to stop the Mongols from attacking. Möngke killed a pro-Mongol Korean general named Lee Hyeong and his family in protest. His military general, Jalairtai, then destroyed lands and the buildings in Goryeo as punishment. Many of the peasants of Goryeo surrendered due to despair and famine.

In 1258, the Choe clan wanted to continue the war against the Mongols, despite the overwhelming odds. However, a political party within Goryeo called upon the literati party, which was against the war, to stage a counter-coup and assassinate the head of the Choe clan. The literati party was a group of scholars protected by clan members, and it was their function to render political advice based on their studies and wisdom. Upon their advice, the head of the Choe clan was assassinated, and a peace treaty was made with the Mongols. King Gojong sent his heir, Wonjong, as a hostage. Also, as part of the agreement between Goryeo and the Mongols, the king of Goryeo had to marry a Mongolian princess and be subservient to their Mongol overlords. For their part, the Mongols guaranteed autonomy to Goryeo with Wonjong at its head, as King Gojong died the next year in 1259. However, Goryeo had to agree to become a vassal state of the Mongols.

In 1271, the Yuan Dynasty under the fifth khagan, or leader of the Mongols, Kublai Khan, was established. They adopted a Chinese-style administration but retained some of their Mongolian practices and were never totally Sinicized. The Mongolian aristocracy and the members of the Goryeo royal family intermarried over the years for the sake of unity.

In the late 13th century, the history of the Yuan Dynasty and Goryeo overlapped. Kublai Khan was expansionistic and sought to conquer the Song Dynasty in China and the islands of Japan.

Goryeo-Mongolian Relations

In 1274, after King Wonjong of Goryeo died, his heir, Chungnyeol, married Kublai Khan's daughter, Jangmok. That union brought the Korean Peninsula into a period of Mongolization, as the court system was now set up according to the administrative hierarchy of the Yuan Dynasty. The intermarriages continued throughout the imperial line. Ordinary, non-imperial people of Goryeo, the common people, along with the Han Chinese, was the largest subculture in China at the time.

The tribute Goryeo paid to the Mongols consisted of gold, silver, textiles, grain, ginseng, and falcons. In terms of personnel, the Koreans provided soldiers, eunuchs, palace women, and Buddhist monks. Goryeo concubines also serviced the Mongolian aristocrats.

The Mongols had already swallowed up mainland China in addition to Goryeo, but it was determined to spread its empire to Japan. In 1274, Kublai Khan demanded the skills of the Goryeo shipbuilders and weapon craftsmen to provide his forces with supplies to conduct an invasion. A large number of the Goryeo men were pressed into service as ground troops and seamen. Goryeo supplied as many as 770 ships, all fully manned, and 5,000 ground forces. That number increased to 10,000 infantrymen, and they were equipped with 900 ships to make an amphibious landing on Japan. However, the effort failed. Kublai tried again in 1281, but it failed due to a typhoon. In the same year, Kublai's favorite wife died, and he became despondent. In addition, the Yuan Dynasty ran into severe financial difficulties brought on by corruption and the perennial expenditures of wars. In 1294, Kublai Khan died. He was succeeded by nine short-lived khans until the ascendancy of Toghon Temür.

Much friction occurred when Toghon Temür fell in love with Lady Ki, a Korean concubine. Mongolian emperors were expected to marry only Mongolian women, so when he tried to promote Lady Ki to the status of secondary wife, it gave rise to much public resentment. In 1339, Lady Ki gave birth to a son, which allowed Toghon Temür to grant Lady Ki the status he wanted to give her. This son, Ayushiridara, was named as his heir. Lady Ki was politically manipulative and steadily worked toward getting not only members of her family into positions of power but also other people from Goryeo.

In 1354, one of the Mongol generals led an attack against the Red Turbans, a group that sought to curtail the power of the Mongols. Toghon Temür was terrified that this general would use his strength to crush the Yuan Dynasty, which had become weakened over the years, so he suddenly dismissed him. This might have helped him gain some power back, but it also meant that Toghon Temür had to rely on local warlords for assistance in military affairs.

When Toghon Temür lost interest in politics soon after, his son, Ayushiridara, known as Biligtü Khan, sought to gain power. He had become the crown prince in 1353, but despite his title, he came into conflict with Toghon Temür's aides, who held the real power of the empire. The Yuan Dynasty began to crumble at this stage, and it was overthrown by the Ming Dynasty of China in 1368, freeing China and Korea from Mongol rule. The Northern Yuan Dynasty was then formed, which was based in the Mongolian Plateau.

Red Turban Rebellion (1351–1368)

The Red Turban army was founded by Guo Zixing and included followers of the White Lotus, a religious movement that was popular among the Han Chinese. The rebellions were small and sporadic, at least to begin with, and they sought to wrest China away from the control of the Mongols. The country was being victimized by natural disasters, famine, and poverty, and so, the Chinese concluded that their Mongol overlords had lost the "mandate of heaven," meaning divine approval.

When King Gongmin of Goryeo noted the efforts of the Chinese to rid the mainland of the Mongols and the remnants of the Yuan Dynasty, Gongmin wanted to do the same in Goryeo. He removed all pro-Mongol officials, nobles, and military personnel who were pro-Mongolian. In 1356, his army annexed the provinces of northern Goryeo, which had been totally occupied by the Mongols. However, in 1359, the Red Turbans invaded Goryeo and retook the northern provinces, along with its capital city, Pyongyang. They were soon after pushed out of the city.

After this, the Red Turbans wanted to place the peninsula of Goryeo under Chinese control and subsume them into the future Ming Dynasty. In 1360, General Choe Yeong put down the Red Turbans. Choe Yeong became very popular when he appointed himself mayor of Pyongyang and increased crop production, staving off the hunger of the populace.

When she saw the growing strength of Choe Yeong, Lady Ki (now Empress Ki) of the declining Yuan Dynasty sent in troops under Choe Yu to overthrow Goryeo. Choe Yeong, however, defeated the Mongol troops, which were the last vestiges of the Yuan regime. Yeong thus established the independence of the Goryeo Dynasty by 1364.

In 1368, back in China, the Red Turban Rebellion was victorious, and their leader, Zhu Yuanzhang, established the Ming Dynasty.

Chapter 4 – The Joseon Dynasty of Goryeo

Having purged the government of the Mongols, King Gongmin of Goryeo sought to establish relations with the Ming Dynasty of China, but the bureaucracy faulted him for wanting to do so. They wanted an independent Goryeo because they were afraid of losing their status. In 1374, King Gongmin was assassinated by his wife and her lover. His son, U, also written as Woo, became the next king of Goryeo at the age of eleven.

In 1388, with the support of King U, General Choe Yeong decided to attempt to invade the Liaodong Peninsula, a peninsula in northeast China. Yi Seong-gye, also known as Yi Dan, who was a colleague of Choe Yeong's during the Red Turban invasion, strenuously advised against such a move, stating that the Ming were much stronger than Goryeo and that it was also against the Confucian way of thinking. In addition, Goryeo would be vulnerable to Japanese pirates and the upcoming monsoon season. Yi, who had been chosen to lead the invasion, refused to commit his troops and returned south.

Instead, Yi Seong-gye went to the capital and defeated the forces there that were still loyal to the king, which were led by Choe Yeong. Yi enjoyed a lot of popularity among government officials and the general populace, so it wasn't too difficult for him to eliminate his opponent, Choe Yeong. Instead of seizing power for himself, Yi Seong-gye gave the throne to King U's son, Chang. A little over a year later, Yi Seong-gye poisoned both U and Chang, giving the throne to one more ruler, Gongyang, before seizing it for himself in 1392.

Yi wanted to keep the name Goryeo for the country but was persuaded to change it. Yi Seong-gye then chose the name Joseon for the new dynasty, which had been a name for a previous state, and he became known by the name of Taejo of Joseon—not to be confused with his namesake, Taejo, who ruled Goryeo in the 10th century.

The Vicious Dispute over Succession

As his first task, Taejo sent envoys to the Ming Dynasty of China, Japan, the Ryukyu Kingdom—an archipelago that lay to the south—and Siam (Thailand). His capital city was Hanseong, current-day Seoul.

As his second task, Taejo decided that the line of succession should be determined in view of the fact that he had eight sons. His fifth son, Yi Bang-won, would have been the most logical choice because he contributed a lot to establishing the organization of the new government. However, it was a well-known fact that Bang-won held animosity toward Taejo's prime minister, Jeong Do-jeon, so Taejo chose his youngest son, Yi Bang-seok, as his heir. Jeong Do-jeon supported his choice as well. After Taejo's wife died, Jeong Do-jeon sought to kill the other sons of Taejo in order to secure his position. However, Yi Bang-won heard of this plan, and in 1398, he killed Jeong Do-jeon, his followers, and two sons of the late queen, including the crown prince. Taejo was aghast that his son, Yi Bang-won, would kill his brothers, so he then chose his second son, Yi Bang-gwa, later known as King Jeongjong, as his heir apparent. Taejo retired soon after.

King Jeongjong was more easily intimidated by Yi Bang-won than his father had been, and he gave the crown to Yi Bang-won in 1400 after a successful rebellion by his forces. King Taejo, who was still alive, held on to the royal seal and refused to recognize Yi Bang-won, who assumed the throne under the name Taejong. This didn't stop Yi Bang-won from becoming king, though, and when King Taejo died in 1408, there was nothing left to stop King Taejong.

Administrative Changes

As one of his first acts, King Taejong abolished the private armies maintained by the aristocrats. This created a pool of trained soldiers with whom he could set up a national army. His second action was to reform taxation. During the process of determining land ownership, he discovered land that was hidden from authorities so the owners could escape paying taxes. Once that subterfuge was uncovered, it greatly increased the national treasury. In addition, Taejong closed many of the temples that were formerly constructed by the Goryeo kings, which increased the size of the treasury as well.

In 1399, King Taejong started converting Joseon into an absolute monarchy. He replaced the governmental body, the Dopyeong Assembly, with a state council that approved of the king's various edicts. Those who disobeyed his rulings were either killed or exiled.

Taejong also promoted a new brand of Confucianism and tailored it to emphasize government, military service, and civic responsibility. Neo-Confucianism promotes an orderly society guided by people whose positions are awarded on the basis of merit, not birth. During the 14th century, Buddhism had fallen into disrepute as corruption and greed grew among the Buddhist monks and their followers.

Gunpowder

For years, potassium nitrate, also known as saltpeter, was used as an elixir in China. During the course of developing medications using saltpeter, explosive properties were accidentally discovered during the manufacturing process whenever it was mixed with sulfur and charcoal. Flames and fire erupted, often burning the hands and faces of the alchemists. In time, they utilized the mixture for its explosive properties. During the Mongol invasions, it was attached to arrows, creating "flying fire." In 1350, it was put into rudimentary Chinese cannons, which would propel a projectile, helping to annihilate the Mongol troops. The Song Dynasty of China attempted to keep this invention secret, but soon, the process was replicated by troops in Joseon as well.

Between 1374 and 1376, a scientist by the name of Choe Museon visited China and bribed a Chinese scientist to give him the recipe for gunpowder. He then developed a technique to extract potassium nitrate from the soil, which is composed of decaying matter. Following that, he developed something called the *hwacha*, a device that was similar to the first modern multiple rocket launchers. The *hwacha* was used effectively in future clashes with the enemy, most notably during the Battle of Jinpo, which was against the Japanese.

Sejong the Great (r. 1418–1450)

King Taejong retired as king in 1418, but he still ruled as a regent with his son, Sejong. Following the Neo-Confucian philosophy of an organized and obedient society, King Sejong strengthened the military. In 1430, he established a new taxation system, but before doing so, he first distributed a poll to assess public opinion. It was a great way for him to provide equality throughout the land, and 57 percent of the respondents approved of the system he proposed. He also was one of the first to grant maternity and paternity leaves.

Agricultural Innovations

King Sejong commissioned two books on agriculture tailored to meet the needs of the soil and climate in Joseon. The most famous book is called *Nongsa jikseol*, or *Straight Talk on Farming*. The conditions that could be artificially created in order to raise rice under the different conditions in Joseon was elucidated. In his book, he talked about how to grow rice in irrigated lowland wetlands and the rainfed deep-water uplands, as well as the utilization of particular drought-resistant species of rice for growth in the dry uplands and the cultivation of rice during the rainy seasons. Trade with Ming China aided the two countries in establishing a market for the sale of seed varieties that were drought-resistant.

The writers also cover the most efficient uses of the ecosystems in Joseon for the production of two different kinds of millet—glutinous and foxtail millet—as well as the cultivation of soybeans, red beans, mung beans, barley, buckwheat, and sesame. The book also describes crop rotation as a means to permit the soil to replenish itself.

Sejong, who was very sensitive to agricultural disasters, such as droughts, extended allowances to farmers whose crops were affected by unexpected environmental occurrences. He also distributed food to those who were in need during times of economic stress.

Inventions

King Sejong appreciated skill and talent, regardless of one's social status. Around 1430, he promoted Jang Yeong-sil to a position that qualified him to work at the royal palace. In 1433, he developed a celestial globe, an instrument that could use the positions of heavenly objects throughout the year to predict the best growing seasons and to tell time. As he refined the design, Joseon astronomers were able to plot the course of seven visible planets as well as the sun, moon, and the stars. In 1434, the scientists at Jiphyeonjeon, a royal research institute, invented a better metal printing press, the first one having been invented by Choe Yun-ui of Goryeo in 1234. Jang also created sundials and a water clock, the latter being based on a crude Chinese model from the 11ᵗʰ century. Some of these inventions made during this time flowed from Sejong's focus on agriculture. Jang invented the *cheugugi*, Korea's first rain gauge, in 1441, which would later be used for gathering data on the precipitation in the country. Jang also invented the *supyo* in 1441, which was the world's first water gauge.

Language

King Sejong hired scholars on a regular basis and had them work in what was called the Hall of Worthies, also known as the aforementioned Jiphyeonjeon. One of his assignments for them was to develop the first Joseon alphabet, which is known as hangul. Before the creation of this alphabet, Koreans used Classical Chinese alongside their own native writing systems. This meant that many lower-class Koreans were illiterate, as there was a huge difference between the Chinese and Korean languages. In 1443, the institute created a manual for the new language, titled *Hunminjeongeum* (or, in English, *The Proper Sounds for the Education of the People*), and distributed it to all of the people. The language that King Sejong promulgated used far less alphabetic characters than the Chinese. Even the lower classes could master this new language, and they started becoming literate, much to the annoyance of the elites who wanted to be seen as in a class above and apart from the common people.

King Sejong himself was a poet, and the most famous poem attributed to him is *Songs of the Flying Dragon,* written in 1445. An excerpt:

The stream whose source is deep

Gushes forth even in a drought.

It forms a river

And gains the sea.

Death and Succession Crisis

In 1450, Sejong died after suffering complications from diabetes. He had appointed his eldest son, Munjong, to succeed him. Munjong was sickly, so Sejong accompanied that appointment with a further successor, his grandson, Danjong, whom he placed under the protection of the members of the Hall of Worthies. As Sejong had foreseen, Munjong didn't live long (only two years), and so, Danjong succeeded him. However, Danjong was only twelve years old, and that gave rise to a usurpation of the throne by his uncle, Sejo, in 1455.

Six scholars then wove a plot to have Danjong returned to the throne. However, one of the conspirators, Gim Jil, betrayed his associates from the Hall of Worthies and revealed the conspiracy to his father-in-law, who told King Sejo. Although he wanted to forgive them, even attempting to have them repent of their deeds and acknowledge his legitimacy, he realized they never would truly submit and had them executed. More than seventy people were put to death during this time, including Danjong. He also eliminated the Hall of Worthies altogether, but he did keep Gim Jil alive, whom he awarded with high-level positions. Eventually, Gim became the governor of Gyeongsang Province in southeastern Joseon.

King Sejo (r. 1455–1468)

King Sejo tightened the monarchy and further advanced legal organization by passing the Grand Code for State Administration, which was specifically designed for dynastic rulers to serve as a guide. The code contained laws regulating a system for the enforcement of a criminal code along with some portions devoted to contract law, finance, and civil matters. It wasn't actually put into effect until 1474 when it was completed under the reign of his successors.

The Joseon Dynasty and the Jianzhou Invasions

The Jurchen people had clashed with Korea back in the 12th century. In 1460 and 1470, one of the subdivisions of this tribe, the Jianzhou, intruded on the northern borders of Joseon. They crossed the borders of northern Joseon to obtain ginseng for trade, but they also attacked Joseon villages, mostly for the purpose of confiscating the red ginseng crop grown in that region. Red ginseng was highly sought after by the Chinese, who could only grow a limited amount.

Red ginseng has a long and illustrious history as a medicinal herb and was said to be an aphrodisiac, having properties that increase longevity, reduce stress, and increase vitality. The Joseon variety was a very profitable crop. It is no longer grown there, but single roots from which red ginseng were made from have been auctioned off in the modern day for as high as $50,000!

The Violent Regencies of the Joseon Queens

King Sejo died in 1468 and was succeeded by his son, Yejong, whose mother, Queen Jeonghee, the wife of Sejo, ruled in his place, as he was too sickly to rule. During her regency, farmers were granted many of the lands formerly owned by the military in order to increase agricultural production. Yejong and his mother only ruled for a year. Following his reign, Yeong's nephew, Seongjong, became the next king. He was also too young to rule (he was only twelve), and so, his grandmother, Queen Jeonghee, and his mother, Queen Insu, ruled in his stead until he was nineteen -years old.

King Seongjong added some improvements to the law of the land that was first developed by King Sejo. Despite some future revisions, this code was the longest-lasting legal code in Korean history.

Land ownership became extremely important during Seongjong's reign, not only as a source of taxes but also as an opportunity for leases and a way for peasants to produce crops. Status was now becoming attached to land ownership, and some larger estates were created. The legal codes were also expanded to regulate land ownership and rights.

Seongjong was a scholarly and religious man, and he restored Neo-Confucianism after Buddhism underwent a resurgence in 1462 due to Chinese influences; the resurgence was also influenced by his wife, Jeonghyeon, who was incredibly devoted to Buddhism. The Hall of Worthies, which had been eradicated around 1456, morphed into the Hall of Leave of Study, which young scholars could attend. Due to King Seongjong's intellectual pursuits, there was a resurgence of literature and book publishing.

However, disputes did occur under Seongjong's prosperous rule. When Seongjong's first wife died, he married Yun. This made her Seongjong's second wife, and they had a son named Yi Yung.

However, King Seongjong also had sexual relations with his concubines, which was, of course, permissible. Yun became insanely jealous of them. On one occasion, historians wrote that she had his concubines followed. Furious about these relationships, she attacked the king and even scratched his face with her sharp fingernails, leaving scars, and it is said that she even poisoned one of the concubines in 1477. Queen Yun was then deposed as regent and exiled. However, she didn't change her ways while in exile, and influential officials asked for her execution. She died in 1482, after having been poisoned.

In 1494, Sejong was then succeeded by his son, Yi Yung, now known as Yeonsangun. Upon his ascension to the throne, Yeonsangun discovered what happened to his mother and became wildly enraged. He opened an intensive investigation into her execution and interrogated all the palace personnel that served at the time. As his temper rose during these investigations, he transferred his hatred to many of the women and officials who were serving in the palace. When one of the scholars wrote a history that indicated King Sejo usurped the throne, it pushed Yeonsangun over the edge. He purged the government of scholars during the First Literati Purge in 1498, brutally executing some and exiling others.

The purges weren't over, however. In 1504, the details of his mother's death were revealed to him, which greatly upset him. He promptly responded to this news by beating two of his father's concubines to death, as well as ordering the execution of those officials who had supported his mother's death. At least 36 officials were killed by forcing them to drink poison, and eight of these bodies were mutilated. This number doesn't even include the families of the officials, who were also punished. During this time, he got into a fight with his grandmother, Queen Insu, and pushed her, killing her.

The rest of Yeonsangun's rule was very cruel, although it should be noted that the beginning of his reign before he discovered the truth about his mother was fairly stable. He converted the royal university into his own pleasure grounds, and he demolished a large residential area in the capital to build hunting grounds, displacing 20,000 residents. After the people began to mock him in hangul, he decided to ban the use of the alphabet. And his rough treatment extended to the nobility and government officials as well; he even executed a minister for accidentally spilling a drink when he poured it into Yeonsangun's cup.

Seeing that Yeonsangun's insane cruelty seemed to know no bounds, court officials conspired against him. In 1506, he was deposed and sent into exile on Ganghwa Island. His half-brother, Jungjong, replaced him. Jungjong wanted to return to the kind of Joseon Seongjong oversaw, but he was limited in his movements, as the coup leaders who placed him on the throne supervised his moves. Once they died, though, Jungjong began to assert his authority.

Jungjong very much favored the philosophies taught by the more liberal Confucian scholars, but very powerful political leaders within the government squelched what they considered to be improper philosophies. Jungjong, in particular, followed the teachings of Jo Gwang-jo, a scholar who promoted equality between the rich and the poor and who believed that officials could even be appointed from the lower classes. The older members of the administration were particularly afraid of the growing popularity of Jo's brand of Neo-Confucianism. Jo Gwang-jo quickly moved through the ranks, and officials who disliked him began to plant the seeds of doubt in Jungjong's mind, saying that another coup could be possible with Jo Gwang-jo behind it this time. This started the Third Literati Purge, which began in 1519. Jo Gwang-jo did not see any of this coming and was exiled due to a massive outpouring of support for Jo Gwang-jo's innocence by his students. However, Jungjong wanted him dead, and in 1520, he was forced to drink poison. By 1521, 225 officials had been affected by the purge, and most of Jo's reforms, which promoted equality between the classes, had been rescinded.

The Three Offices

These offices existed in the earlier Goryeo Dynasty but were expanded under Seongjong's reign. It was Seongjong's hope that the Neo-Confucian scholars, called the Sarim, would check the power of the ministers, the Hungu. These two constantly fought with each other, and this conflict played a major role in the literati purges. Although the purges are thought to be due to these rival factions, some believe the kings of Joseon wanted to weaken the Three Offices, as they balanced out their rule. Below is a definition of the offices.

Office of Inspector General

This office was in charge of licensing inspectors and officials, impeachment, legal questions, and the proper behavior of the king's relatives. Additionally, it maintained Confucian order in the hierarchy of government. Admission to this office required a thorough background check.

Office of Censors

The Office of Censors had the delicate responsibility to advise the king if he wished to promulgate a policy or issue a decree. They didn't have the authority to pass a decree but could confer with the Office of Inspector General in terms of presenting a modification or preventing the passage of an improper mandate or decree. This group worked closely with the public press, especially in terms of the proper wording of official decrees.

Office of Special Advisors

This group monitored the content of the royal libraries and weighed the beliefs of Neo-Confucianism against the content of the documents present.

The Fourth Literati Purge

Jungjong died in 1544, and the crown prince Injong became king. However, he died eight months later, and the son of Jungjong's third wife, Myeongjong, became king. The chronicles seem to implicate Queen Munjeong in Injong's death, as they record that the queen was often visited by a spirit of the night and was haunted by the voice of the deceased child. She woke up screaming many nights. In mortal fear and terror, Queen Munjeong became so perturbed about it that she moved the palace.

Now, Jungjong's second wife, who had given birth to Injong, had a brother named Yun Im, while Queen Munjeong had a brother named Yun Won-hyeong. Each brother was very ambitious and formed their own political power groups. Yun Im's group was known as the Lesser Yun faction, and they were progressives. Yun Won-hyeong's group, the Greater Yun faction, was conservative. Geographically, members of the conservative faction mostly lived west of the capital, and the progressive element lived east of the capital. These divisions further split into subdivisions—the northerners, the southerners, and the eastern and western sections near the capital.

In 1545, there was an enormous shake-up of the political factions, and the Fourth Literati Purge took place. As a result, Yun Im was executed, along with some Confucian scholars. Many historians assert that the Yun Won-hyeong faction created a plot to have him executed.

The political feuds of the 15th and 16th centuries created military vulnerability because the size and strength of the army was often an item on the political agenda. During the reign of King Myeongjong's successor, King Seonjo, the conservative faction was in power, and reforms were slowed down. One of those reforms promoted an increase of the military to defend the country against the Jurchens along the border, as well as against Japan, which was becoming a formidable force in the area. However, the conservatives resisted a defensive buildup, and it led to their own undoing when other countries, like Japan, took advantage of that exposure.

Chapter 5 – Foreign Invasions

Six-Year War with Japan

In 1590, one of the most powerful daimyos of Japan, Toyotomi Hideyoshi, emerged as the primary military leader who united the clan factions within the country, allowing Japan to stand on its own. To keep the country from falling into civil war and to expand Japanese territory, Hideyoshi had plans to conquer China. He increased his military and naval strength in preparation. Then he contacted King Seonjo of Joseon, asking permission to enter into China through the peninsula. Through word he received back from the traders, Seonjo discovered this military buildup and wanted to determine Hideyoshi's real intentions for making that request. Therefore, Seonjo sent emissaries from both Joseon political parties to Hideyoshi to clarify the matter. They returned and reported to the king that Hideyoshi wanted to attack the Ming Dynasty in China. The letter Hideyoshi sent with the ambassadors asked Korea to submit to Japan and join them in the war against China.

Joseon had a long-standing, positive relationship with the Ming and realized that he shouldn't yield to Hideyoshi's demand, so he turned him down. However, Joseon had been weakened militarily during the prior years of internal conflicts. Seonjo's strongest naval commander, Yi Sun-sin, rushed to prepare for battle. He trained military forces and had warships built, including a newly invented ship called a "turtle ship," which was an iron-clad vessel equipped with artillery.

In May of 1592, Japan sent over 150,000 men to Pusan, also known as Busan, a port city on the southern coast of Joseon. At sea, the Joseon navy couldn't halt the initial advance but managed to scatter the naval reinforcement fleets. They also sunk 63 Japanese ships and blocked vessels carrying supplies.

The Japanese forces that did land raged throughout the southern regions, burning and looting as they moved northward toward Seoul. The people in Seoul virtually abandoned the capital, which included King Seonjo, who fled to Pyongyang, which is now the capital of North Korea.

The Japanese occupied both Seoul and Pyongyang before moving eastward toward the sea. Japan had planned not only on its supply ships but also on crops that could be confiscated locally. However, because of Joseon's amazing success at sea, that plan failed.

The Joseon people were furious at the government's failure to protect the country, so they organized a voluntary militia. What especially motivated them were the atrocities that the Japanese soldiers inflicted upon them. Scholars, civilians, and peasants were slaughtered. It was customary for the Japanese in those days to prove their valor on the battlefield by cutting off heads of those they killed. In the Korean invasions, due to the number of civilians killed, it was easier to transport noses instead of heads. The Mimizuka, or Ear Mound, is a monument in Japan that preserves at least 38,000 noses of the Koreans killed during the invasions.

In January of 1593, Ming China sent a force of around 40,000 men to join up with the Joseon forces; they attacked the Japanese stationed at Seoul and retook Pyongyang. However, when the Ming forces were defeated at the Battle of Byeokjegwan on February 27th, 1593, the Ming retreated, leaving the Koreans stranded. Regardless, the Joseon and the Chinese still had a mountain redoubt in Haengju in the north, and the forces there fought courageously, losing many men. The Japanese staged nine successive attacks there but were forced to retreat each time. This battle greatly improved Korean morale.

At the Siege of Jinju Fortress in July of that year, the Japanese broke down the dikes that held back the moat. They were met with punishing volleys of arrows and had to pull back, though. The Japanese then dragged in siege towers but were forced to back off because of the cannon fire from atop the battlements. It was a prolonged battle and lasted seven days. On the third day, General Kim Si-min was killed, along with many other Korean soldiers. Nevertheless, the hearty Koreans fought onward. The ladders the Japanese put up against the walls were smashed by the Korean defensive forces. Eventually, the Japanese mined sections of the wall. As it was raining intensely, sections of the wall weakened, and the Japanese were finally able to take possession of the fort. Today, there is an annual festival, the Jinju Namgang Yudeung Festival, commemorating the lives of the 70,000 Koreans slaughtered in this fierce conflict.

By this point in the war, the Japanese invasion force, which had started out with 150,000 men, were down to about 53,000. With more Chinese coming in every day as reinforcements, as well as the cold winter that brought about hunger and frostbite, the Japanese retreated to the coast. The two sides remained at a stalemate for several months, as both sides were unwilling to make any offensive moves.

The Japanese also lost a number of minor battles, and the Japanese general, Konishi Yukinaga, withdrew most of his forces and sued for peace. However, because the Ming had pulled out of Joseon, the deluded Japanese thought they'd won! The Ming felt the same way, as they had recaptured Pyongyang and the Joseons had taken the Haengu fortress and destroyed half of the Japanese fleet. Therefore, Ming China insisted Japan become its vassal state. An exchange of hostages was discussed but were never agreed to, and negotiations dragged on for three years with no resolution.

In February of 1597, the Japanese invaded Joseon a second time with around 141,000 troops. They landed at Pusan, as they had done in the previous conflict. This time, however, Joseon was much better prepared. The Ming also sent around 55,000 troops to help deal with the invasion. Initially, the Japanese were largely confined to Gyeongsang Province in southeastern Joseon. Because of their "slash-and-burn" techniques, virtually all of Gyeongsang Province became a wasteland. Thousands of Koreans were killed, with famine and disease followed that. The Ming were not much better; they did not distinguish between loyal Joseon civilians and those who supported the Japanese. The Joseon armies themselves often forcefully acquired food and supplies from civilians; as is typical in most warfare, the civilians got the worst of it.

Between 1597 and 1598, the Koreans demonstrated that they had become far more proficient in battle tactics than in 1593. In the Battle of Myeongnyang, the Joseon cleverly constructed multiple-level warships called panokseons, which used both rowers and a sail. The panokseons had flat bottoms, as the waters around Korea could be deceivingly shallow. The Myeongnyang Strait was especially tricky because it was incredibly narrow, and a sudden change of the tide could catch a sea captain unprepared. The Joseon, of course, used that knowledge to their advantage by luring in the clumsier Japanese warships. Joseon Admiral Yi Sun-sin was manning the flagship at the north end of the strait, and the numerous Japanese ships rushed in. Once the tide changed, however, the Japanese fleet started drifting backward, colliding into each other! As would happen in any narrow channel, the rapidity of the current can become treacherous, and many who tried to swim ashore in the chaos drowned.

The Siege of Ulsan, which lasted from January 29th to February 19th, 1598, represented a significant loss for Joseon, as they were overwhelmingly outnumbered by the Japanese once an unexpected contingent of reinforcements arrived. The Joseon wanted to capture the fortress of Ulsan from the Japanese, and the initial vanguard did manage to force the Japanese to seek shelter in the inner chambers as they were attacked by climbers. However, the fact that Ulsan was built on higher ground gave the Japanese a distinct topographical advantage. The Joseon troops had cannons, but the range was too short for the cannon fire to reach, so Inspector-General Yang Hao was forced to withdraw his men.

Joseon really craved another Japanese fort, though, and in the fall of 1598, they attempted to conquer the garrison at Suncheon. They tried tempting the Japanese commander, Konishi Yukinaga, and some of his forces out into the open under the pretext of negotiations. The Joseon troops miscalculated the timing and opened their cannon fire too soon, sending the Japanese scurrying back into the shelter of the fort. The Chinese allies, who weren't as familiar with the Korean waters, sent in ships. However, those ships became jammed in the shallow waters, and Joseon lost the battle.

Yi Sun-sin had been in charge of the navy, but he suspected he was being lured into an ambush after receiving orders to go after the Japanese, as the tip was from a Japanese spy. Thus, he held back from attacking them, but he displeased the king in doing so. As a result, he was removed from duty and replaced by Won Gyun. However, Won Gyun proved to be incompetent when compared to Yi Sun-sin, losing the Battle of Chilcheollyang and incurring a heavy loss of Joseon ships, as well as his own life. Quickly, Yi Sun-sin was reinstated. With only 12 ships and 200 seamen, he gained the advantage, utilizing his expert knowledge of the tides and currents. At the Battle of Noryang in December 1598, however, Yi Sun-sin was killed. Despite that, the Joseon/Ming fleet achieved a tremendous victory. The Japanese forces, which were heavily decimated, returned home to find out that the Japanese shogun, Toyotomi Hideyoshi, had died in September, his death being kept a secret so as not to squash the army's morale.

Following the Japanese invasion, the Joseon established a policy of isolationism. King Seonjo felt that trade with the Chinese was sufficient enough and that too much foreign interference only brought bloodshed and devastation.

Bloody Factionalism Continues

King Seonjo keenly felt the effects of the horrendous war with the Japanese, having to deal with the starvation of his people and the loss of acres of farmland. He gave free grain to families in need and tried to reconstruct Joseon but was thwarted by the terrible economic conditions. In 1608, he died, passing the crown to his second son, Gwanghaegun. Gwanghaegun took the throne during a particularly violent period of party politics. He also commanded little respect because he was the son of Seonjo's concubine, which was against Confucian beliefs.

As soon as he ascended to the throne, the small faction of northern conservatives conspired to stage a coup to make Gwanghaegun's brother, Yeong-chang, king. The plot was exposed, however, and its leader was executed. Yeong-chang was arrested and died the following year. The larger conservative faction, called the Greater Northerner faction, removed many officials from the opposing party from office. They also stripped Queen Inmok, Yeong-chang's mother, of her title and threw her into prison. His grandfather was also found guilty of treason and executed.

During his reign, King Gwanghaegun attempted to give members of all the factions representation in government but was unsuccessful. In 1623, he was the victim of a coup and was sent into exile. Injo, the grandson of King Seonjo, was then put on the throne by the ultra-conservative Westerner faction.

The Manchu Invasions

In the early 17th century, the more aggressive branch of the troublesome Jurchen people (the Jianzhou Jurchens) migrated to the northeastern region of China in the country now known as Manchuria. Their dynasty was called the Later Jin Dynasty, which eventually evolved into the Qing Dynasty.

In 1618, Nurhaci, the king of the Jurchens, declared war against the Ming Dynasty as well as those allied with them, that is, Joseon. Nurhaci wrote to King Injo of Joseon, condemning him for his association with the Ming Dynasty. Nurhaci justified himself by writing that Heaven had chosen him and his people as the rightful heads of both the Chinese and, therefore, the Koreans. He said:

> Heaven takes me as right and the Nikan, the Han Chinese people, as wrong. The Nikan emperor of the big kingdom also lives under the unchanging word of Heaven. However, the Nikan emperor violated Heaven's rules, going against Heaven, and making other nations suffer for it.

Nurhaci's rationale was rooted in shamanistic legend, which he used to his advantage. Historians, though, said that Nurhaci was actually seeking revenge for the deaths of his father and grandfather in an earlier battle with the Ming.

In 1627, Hong Taiji, who took over after Nurhaci, invaded Joseon. The Jurchen forces were composed mostly of Jurchen tribal warriors, and they first attacked the northern garrisons of Neunghan and Anju. Although Ming China sent some troops to help stave off the attack, those two forts fell, as did Pyongyang. The Jurchens then moved toward southern Joseon. King Injo fled from Hanseong (modern-day Seoul) and sued for peace. However, Hong Taiji complained that Joseon was still aiding the Ming people after a Joseon general, Mao Wenlong, provided food to the stricken Ming soldiers there. Furthermore, after the hostilities stopped, Mao and the Joseon in the north resumed trade with the Ming. The Jurchens insisted that Joseon break all relations with the Ming, and they did so. The Joseon authorities later executed General Wenlong for his "treachery." Injo's successor, Hyojong, honored the terms, although he sometimes wanted to take revenge.

In 1635, Hong Taiji changed the name of his people from Jurchens to Manchus in order to distance themselves from the Jianzhou Jurchens, who were ruled over by the Chinese. Since the Later Jin

Dynasty was a reference to the Jurchen people, the nobles of the Manchus recommended that Hong Taiji establish a new dynasty in China. He did so in 1636, calling it the Qing Dynasty, with Hong Taiji as its first emperor. King Injo and many of the people in Joseon who were still loyal to the old Ming dynasty took that as an offense and agitated the people against the Qing Dynasty. In fact, when some Manchu delegates visited Joseon, the king refused to acknowledge them. The Manchu were incensed at that affront, as was the newly installed Qing emperor.

In 1636, Hong Taiji led Manchu, Mongolian, and Han Chinese warriors against Joseon. Manchu Prince Yu, also known as Dodo, led a huge division of 30,000 men, and Hong Taiji led the main division with 70,000 men. They attacked the formidable Namhan Mountain Fortress in order to prevent King Injo from fleeing to Ganghwa Island as other Joseon kings had done in the past. In prior months, however, the king was able to dispatch his consorts and his son to that island for their protection.

There, in the mountainous terrain of northern Joseon, the soldiers of Joseon successfully fended off the Qing invaders with heavy and persistent musket fire. This was only a temporary victory, though. In early 1637, a large force under the command of another Qing prince, Dorgon, assaulted Ganghwa Island, capturing King Injo's son and his wives. Joseon surrendered the following day.

Their agreement with the Qing army consisted of nine requirements:

> 1. Joseon would stop using Ming era name and surrender the Ming seal of investiture.
>
> 2. Joseon would offer his captured sons, Prince Sohyeon and Grand Prince Bontrim, also known as Hyojong, as hostages along with their wives and consorts.
>
> 3. Joseon would accept the Qing calendar.
>
> 4. Joseon would acknowledge the local Ming leaders as their overlords.

5. Joseon would provide men and supplies to aid the Qing army in future fights with the Ming.

6. Joseon would provide warships to the Qing.

7. Joseon wouldn't accept any Ming refugees into their country.

8. The noblewomen of Joseon would intermarry with the Qing.

9. Joseon wouldn't build any more fortresses or castles.

After the surrender of Joseon, atrocities occurred on account of the cruelty of the Qing. Joseon women were kidnapped and raped, and some of the Joseon princesses became concubines for the Qing princes. Because they had had intercourse with the Qing, they were alienated from their families.

While the Joseon prince, Hyojong, was living in Qing China with his wife, Inseon, he learned about many of the advanced military techniques from the Chinese and the Europeans who traded with them. Hyojong was very protective of his brother, Sohyeon, who was the heir to the Joseon throne. In fact, he even went on a Qing campaign to Russia in his brother's place.

It took around forty years for the new Qing Dynasty to assume control over mainland China because of the remaining Ming loyalists in southern China. Prince Sohyeon and Princess Minhoe returned to Joseon about eight years later, and several years after that, Hyojong and his wife did as well.

Since Sohyeon, who was King Ingo's first son and heir, had been in China for years, he returned with many Western scientific ideas and even entertained sympathy for Catholicism, which had grown in some areas of China. The king was horrified by his pro-Western ideas and was furious that Sohyeon had met with the Jesuit missionary Johann Schall von Bell in Beijing. Sohyeon died shortly after returning to Joseon under mysterious circumstances, and historical rumors indicate that the king killed his own son. When

Sohyeon's wife attempted to investigate her husband's death, a story was concocted, possibly by Gwi-in, King Injo's concubine, about Princess Minhoe having committed treason. She was executed, and her three sons were exiled.

Hyojong succeeded Injo in 1649 and attempted to build up the Joseon army with the weapons he had seen in China, hiring some to manufacture muskets for them. However, economic conditions in war-torn Joseon were severe, and he spent much of his reign trying to rebuild and reconstruct his country and died before completing that task. His successor, Hyeonjong, continued that project.

Factionalism Fractures the Royal House

Even while the royal princes were held captive in Qing China, conflicts occurred in Joseon due to the political factions. Arguments and vindictiveness occurred over even the trivial issue about the required length of time for the wearing of mourning attire! When Hyojong died, the Western conservatives felt that only one year was necessary for the wearing of mourning robes by his second wife, Jangryeol, while the Southern faction felt that three years was necessary. In the end, King Hyeonjong made the final decision, which was the one-year period, allowing the Westerners to remain as the major faction.

The Musin Rebellion

In the early 18th century, small splinter groups grew out of the political factions. The Western faction split into the Norons, who followed the Confucian scholar Song Siyeol, and the Sorons, who abided by the teachings of Yun Jeung. In 1724, the Noron faction wanted King Gyeongjong of Joseon to step down in favor of his half-brother, Yeongjo, who favored the Norons. The Soron faction then plotted to assassinate Yeongjo. They didn't need to conspire, however, because Gyeongjong died of food poisoning that was due to the consumption of spoiled shrimp. In fact, historians support this idea, as they state that the king was foolish enough to have consumed seafood that was shipped to him in mid-summer and wasn't kept on ice.

Despite that obvious fact, the Sorons accused Yeongjo of deliberately poisoning the young king. In December 1728, the Musin Rebellion exploded between the two factions. Sim Yu-hyeon and Bak Mi-gwi stole gunpowder, planning to blow up the Hong-hua and Don-hua gates. The fighting between the factions raged on for three weeks, and the government lost control of many of the county seats of the Jeolla Province.

Another literati purge, the Shinim purge, occurred, in which almost all Noron officials lost their positions. Four lost their lives, and 170 were exiled. In 2017, secret letters written by Yeongjo were found, describing the purge. He detested the factional strife that had afflicted his country for years and attempted to put an end to it. He expelled the Sorons from the government and drew the country's attention away from politics. Instead of focusing on politics, King Yeongjo's letters to his people were compassionate.

The country at that time was inundated with frequent rainfalls, destroying many crops. To alleviate their suffering, Yeongjo reduced the taxes and set an example by reducing the size of his own meals. He also initiated many public works projects and encouraged mercantilism and the growth of guilds.

Chapter 6 – Merchants, Farmers, and Foreigners

During the 18th century, commercial wide-scale production of profitable crops, such as ginseng, tobacco, cotton, and, of course, rice, was introduced. New vegetables were grown, such as potatoes, tomatoes, squash, and peppers as a result of the mission spearheaded by Cho Om, who was sent to Japan as an envoy in 1764. Farmer markets became widespread across the countryside. Occupations related to transportation, warehousing, shipbuilding, inn-keeping, and banking flourished. The import-export trade also grew between Joseon and Qing China, and later on with Japan as well. Coins were minted by the thousands, but the upper classes sometimes hoarded them, creating coin shortages, or "coin famines."

Jeong Yakyong aka "Dasan"

The people of Joseon were highly influenced by the versatile thinkers of the age, like Jeong Yakyong, more commonly known as Dasan. He was noted for his Neo-Confucian philosophy, science, law, land reform structures, and government theory. Two of his most famous books, *The Mind of Governing People* and the *Design of Good Government*, focus on the role of government as the means by which a country's people could improve their economic conditions and direct their motivation along a path of righteous and generous behavior. Dasan always stressed the practical aspects of living, as opposed to the esoteric philosophic ramblings of those scholars who argued semantics and etymology. In 1805, Dasan outlined his theoretical methodology for the interpretation of the famous *I Ching,* or "Book of Changes," which is a text on divination that is still used today.

Dasan was exiled from late 1801 until 1818 when Korea discovered that they had as many as 17,000 Korean converts to Catholicism and was threatened by this creeping Western influence. Korea wanted to adhere to a Neo-Confucian philosophy and recognize no other leader than that of the state. In the Western world, the Catholic Church was already a strong political power, and while Dasan wasn't Catholic, his brother was.

The French Invasion

In 1863, King Gojong ascended to the throne. He was still a minor at the time, so his father, Yi Ha-eung, served as regent. His title was the Heungseon Daewongun, meaning "prince of the great court." He was very ambitious, and this was finally an opportunity for him to dominate the political scene. One of his first acts was to fortify the identity of Joseon as a self-determining Neo-Confucian state. Catholicism was considered to be a belief system that was in opposition to Neo-Confucianism, one that polluted the purity of Joseon ideology. Noting that there was a lot of interference in Joseon affairs from French Catholic missionaries, the Daewongun started out by forcibly removing the Catholic leaders and other Joseon Catholics, who had grown to number 23,000 in just a few years.

In January 1866, Russian ships appeared on the eastern coast of Joseon. The Korean Christians saw this as the perfect chance to strengthen their cause and suggested that Joseon join forces with France. The Daewongun seemed to be open to this idea and agreed to meet with Bishop Berneux. But it was just a ploy to get the bishop out in the open; once he arrived in the capital the following month, he was executed. After this, more French missionaries and Korean converts were rounded up.

Because of the execution of the French missionaries, the French consul decided to send a "punitive mission," to Joseon, saying, "Since the kingdom of Joseon killed nine French priests, we shall respond by killing 9,000 Joseon people." The consul made this threat without the authorization of the French government, but France, nevertheless, wanted to open up Joseon to trade.

In 1866, Rear Admiral Pierre-Gustave Roze set off with a small fleet and entered the Han River, which appeared to lead to the capital. Unfortunately, Roze noted that the waters were too shallow for French warships, so he attempted to occupy Ganghwa Island, which was located at the entrance of the Han River, and demanded reparations. The Daewongun was furious, and his fortress on the island held firm. The French troops did manage to invade the royal sanctuary on the mountain there and seized the royal histories and accounting books. Once Roze realized he couldn't make any further progress, though, he retreated.

The *General Sherman* Incident

In 1866, an American ship, the *General Sherman*, was shipwrecked along the Joseon shore. The Americans were concerned about the fate of the vessel but also wanted to use that as an opportunity to chart some of the waters near the peninsula and possibly develop a treaty to handle stranded American sailors. They dispatched the US ambassador to China along with five warships. In June of that year, a small contingent of the Joseon military opened fire upon the Americans. When the Americans requested an apology, none was forthcoming. The US then explained that they were on a peaceful mission, but still, no reply was offered. Like the French had done, the Americans responded with their own "punitive mission." They landed on Ganghwa Island and captured some of the fortresses there. The Joseon military had outdated weapons, and the Americans were able to capture the Joseon ship, the *Sugaki*. Over 200 Joseon troops were killed, along with the first mate of an American warship, the *Colorado*. After the Americans withdrew, the Daewongun further isolated Korea from foreign encroachments. Joseon, however, had very limited success with that, mostly because they were clearly outgunned by foreign forces.

The Tributary System

Ever since Joseon had sworn fidelity to the Qing Empire, Joseon had to pay quarterly tributes to China. It was delivered to the emperor by the Joseon king or his representative, and it consisted of 100 *piculs* (defined as shoulder-weight loads) of rice, 200 *piculs* of white silk, 100 *piculs* of red silk, 100 *piculs* of blue silk, 300 *piculs* of seal skins, 5,000 rolls of paper, and 10 swords. In a week's time, they were allowed to sell the goods to the Chinese public. Up until 1876, Joseon restricted most of their trade to China. Joseon did maintain a cursory relationship with Japan, however, at their outpost in Pusan on the southern coast. In 1854, word raced throughout Joseon about the landing of American ships in Japan that were commanded by Commodore Matthew Perry. These technologically advanced warships were clearly superior to those of Joseon, which intimidated them as the Japanese were forced to sign a treaty that opened up Japan to trade.

In 1873, at the age of 22, the heir to the Joseon throne, Gojong, announced that he was now the fully empowered head of Joseon. His wife, Queen Myeongseong, also known as Queen Min, also gained control over the court, filling high-level positions with her own family members. The Daewongun was upset by this, and he was exiled from the court. There is even a story that Queen Min bricked up his entrance to the palace. She was intelligent, politically astute, and had the tendency to interfere in state affairs. Min coaxed Gojong to initiate military reforms, and King Gojong and Queen Min appealed to the US, which made other Western nations clamor to establish treaties with Joseon.

Japanese Intrusion

Japan sought Asiatic alliances after the American naval presence shook them up. Hurriedly, Japan sought to improve the condition of its own navy. In May 1875, they imitated Perry's arrival by sending out an iron-clad, steam-driven gunboat called the *Un'yo* to Pusan. These negotiations failed, however, and the Japanese returned back to their country.

Shortly thereafter, in September, the *Un'yo* sailed again, this time landing on Ganghwa Island to ask for water and provisions. The forts on the island fired on the Japanese, which they did not take lightly. After firing back, they torched houses and engaged Joseon troops on the island. As their weapons were more advanced, they made short work of the Joseon forces. After this incident, the Japanese navy blockaded the area, demanding an apology from Joseon. Joseon was forced into an unfair treaty with the Japanese in 1876, known as the Treaty of Ganghwa Island. Its stipulations included the following:

> 1. Joseon, later to be known as Korea, was an independent state.
>
> 2. The two countries would exchange envoys within fifteen months.
>
> 3. The port of Pusan and two more seaports would be open to unhindered Japanese trade within a year, along with space for the construction of ancillary buildings and land leases devoted to trade.
>
> 4. Mutual support of stranded Japanese or Korean ships on each other's shores would be offered.
>
> 5. The Japanese would receive immunity from prosecution for crimes committed on Korean soil.

This treaty essentially recognized Korea as a country independent from China, but it was considered an unequal treaty because Japan was afforded many more rights than Korea.

The Imo Incident

In 1881, King Gojong, who had become fascinated with the advancements the Japanese had and sought to make Joseon stronger, hired a Japanese advisor named Horimoto Reizo to help him update his military forces. Military training ensued, but the soldiers were not given their pay in rice for thirteen months. King Gojong, once he learned of the situation, ordered Min Gyeom-ho to pay them. However, he passed the duty onto a steward, who sold the good rice he had been given and gave the soldiers millet mixed with sand.

On July 23rd, 1882, a riot broke out over the matter. Soldiers headed for the home of Min Gyeom-ho, but he was not at home, having learned about the riot ahead of time. This didn't stop them from destroying his home, and after that, they looted weapons and freed political prisoners. Next, the rioters turned their attention on the Japanese, stabbing Horimoto one by one. They turned their attention to the Japanese legation, setting fire to the building. The majority of the people inside managed to make it out, although six Japanese were killed. After this, the rioters moved onto the palace, killing Min Gyeom-ho, as well as other high-ranking officials. They especially wanted to get their hands on Queen Min, but she had managed to escape. The riot was eventually contained, and several officials were executed as a result. However, this incident still damaged relations with the Japanese.

To restrict Japanese involvement in Joseon affairs, the Joseon government had Chinese advisors come in to help with the retraining of their troops. China, however, took advantage of that and started to regain control over Joseon. The Chinese sent in special military advisors and a trade minister, and China also worked out an agreement with Joseon, which resulted in the China-Korea Treaty of 1882. The greatest difficulty with that agreement was the fact that it required Joseon to be a dependency of China.

The Joseon-American Treaty

About a month before the Imo Incident, Joseon had signed a treaty of amity with the United States. It indicated that Joseon was an independent country, that America would take Joseon's side on matters of foreign aggression, and granted Joseon a most-favored-nation status in terms of trade. They invited an American representative to set up a legation, and Lucius Foote was sent to Seoul as America's ambassador there. Upon Gojong's request, America was offered opportunities to invest in railroad construction, streetcars, and even a gold mine.

Aggressive Modernization Begins

Many members of the government were upset with Queen Min's influence; her family supported Chinese influence, something that many in the country were against. When a conflict between France and China broke out, some rebels saw this as the perfect time to stage a coup. In December 1884, a banquet was held to celebrate the opening of the new post office. King Gojong was approached by Kim Ok-gyun, the leader of the Gapsin Coup. He and his followers seized the king and secured protection from the Japanese at the royal palace. With the support of the Japanese, this rebel group issued directives in the king's name and created a program of reform. Some of the points they covered in their program were:

1. Elimination of their tributary relationship with Qing China

2. Cessation of the Confucian model of governance and the introduction of freedom for all classes.

3. A new tax system.

4. Establishment of free enterprise

They then executed six very conservative ministers and replaced them with more progressive statesmen. Their new government only lasted a few days, as the furious Queen Min assembled her own forces. She appealed to China for military support and freed her husband. The newly established reform party disbanded, but nearly all the rebels found refuge in Japan. Kim Ok-gyun was later entreated to come to China, where he was assassinated.

Since the Gapsin Coup was unable to stop the spread of Western influences, Joseon built Western-style hospitals and had consultants come from Western countries, who introduced new agricultural methods, in 1885. In 1886, Joseon obtained a loan from China to build a telegraph from Seoul to Uiju in the northern provinces and later obtained another loan from Germany to expand the telegraph to other major cities.

Russian Agreement

In 1884, Gojong and Queen Min also reached out to Russia for an agreement of amity and the establishment of commerce. China was displeased with that and even considered dethroning King Gojong in response. Joseon then worked on an overland trade agreement with Russia in 1885. Great Britain, alarmed that Joseon was involved in a secret agreement with Russia, then involved itself by making a deal with the Chinese to occupy the Joseon island of Geomundo and fortify it against any intrusions. This wasn't Chinese territory, though, and Joseon objected to this forcibly. Britain withdrew in 1887, but the area became a center of conflict among China, Japan, and Russia, all of whom wanted access to the Tumen River.

Prelude to War

In 1894, a short-lived revolt called the Donghak Rebellion broke out among the peasants, who were being crushed by the growing tax burden. The Japanese troops that were still in Korea moved to suppress the revolt. As they spread around Seoul, Queen Min became alarmed and then prevailed upon her husband to ask for Chinese aid, which he did. In June of 1894, Chinese troops arrived, but Japan asserted that they had violated the Treaty of Tientsin of 1885, which stated that China must notify Japan if they enter Joseon. More Japanese troops were then sent.

Now there were two foreign forces in Joseon—those of Qing China and Imperial Japan. They were on the verge of war, and the first battlefields of the First Sino-Japanese War would be in Joseon.

Chapter 7 – From Independence to Annexation

In July of 1894, Chinese and Japanese forces confronted each other at Aswan, east of Seoul. The Chinese were outnumbered and lost the initial conflict, so they retreated to Pyongyang in the north. By August, the Chinese were defeated in Joseon and moved farther north to the border city of Uiju. They then moved the war to Chinese soil.

Proposed Japanese Reorganization of Joseon

Japan was victorious after the First Sino-Japanese War and decided to control the politics and development of Joseon for the benefit of Japan. The Japanese minister to Joseon, Inoue Kaoru, compelled King Gojong to appoint two pro-Japanese officials to his Cabinet. He then prevailed upon Gojong to establish a new constitution under his guidance called the "Guiding Principles for the Nation." It had eight ministries: 1) foreign affairs, 2) finance, 3) justice, 5) commerce, 6) education, 7) defense, and 8) agriculture.

The Assassination of Queen Min

Japan's interference angered the king and Queen Min, as she always leaned more toward the Chinese. The king himself wasn't that strong, but Queen Min was. So, in 1895, she turned to Russia for help. Two powerful pro-Russian figures were placed on the Cabinet, and two other pro-Japanese ministers were thrown out. A Japanese man, named Miura Goro, had been sent to Joseon as Japan's ambassador with a secret assignment to assassinate Queen Min. Goro gathered a motley group of gangsters, and they killed Queen Min's guards, broke into her bedroom, and dragged her into the yard. There, she was hacked to death, and her body was burned. In fear of his life, King Gojong and his son, Sunjong, fled to the Russian legation, where they stayed for a year.

The Empire of Korea

In 1897, King Gojong returned. Responding to pressure from the Western nations, the country declared itself definitively independent from Japan and China. Gojong announced the establishment of the Empire of Korea, with Gojong as the first emperor.

Under Gojong's leadership, the Gwangmu Reform took place. It rejected the whole old-world order of hierarchical social strata, and its primary goal was social equality. Although many had surnames, those of the lower classes did not. According to this new system, the lower classes would use the names of their masters for themselves or adopt one of the common surnames in the area. The concept of citizenship was also introduced.

Military uniforms were Western-style and were an imitation of the Prussian styles. Diplomats wore Western-style suits, and even the police wore Western-style uniforms.

In 1897, land ownership was no longer determined by the landowners themselves but by outside subcontractors who used modern surveying equipment. In 1898, electricity came to Korea through a partnership between the United States and the Korean Hanseong Electric Company. A telephone network was already in place in 1896, with the first long-distance public phone being installed in 1902.

The educational system was also expanded under this reform, and many were manned by Western missionaries. The Catholic persecutions had ended, and Catholicism had been permitted in the 1880s. Secondary schools were also built by the government, including vocational schools, and private schools were erected as well. However, it wasn't until 1905 that universities were built. A health care system had been established when Korea opened its doors to the world in 1876. Under the Gwangmu Reform, three sectors were more fully fleshed out, which included public health, medical care, and the regulations for licensed medical practitioners.

Russia as Protectorate

Russia drew up a new agreement with Korea in 1898. They wanted Korea to conduct all state affairs through a set of Russian advisors, who would control the financial system and military affairs. The Russians trained the Korean forces and made economic deals with Korea for a long-lasting lumber contract and exclusive mining rights in the mountains. In addition, Korea devoted some of its ports to Russian ships and areas devoted to commercial buildings for Russian commerce. In exchange for those concessions, Russia provided monetary aid. Once any one of those privileges were withdrawn, Russia threatened it would withhold aid. This privileged status inflamed some of the people of Korea, giving rise to protests throughout the country.

Russia had made an agreement with China in late 1897, which allowed Russia access to Port Arthur, an important port city on the tip of the Liaodong Peninsula. Japan, who wanted access to Manchuria and Korea, saw Russia as a threat to their imperial ambitions. And they had good cause to worry because the Russo-Japanese War was looming on the horizon.

Japanese-Russian Buildup to War

In 1903, Russian troops swarmed into Manchuria and planned on using Korea as a bridgehead. Russia manipulated Korea into declaring itself neutral. Japan, however, wanted to keep up some of its influence in Korea, and so, there was a showdown between Japan and Russia over the issue of Korea's non-involvement because of the presence of Russian personnel in the country. Japanese troops were then sent into Seoul and occupied a few government buildings. Korea objected strenuously, so Japan responded by insisting that Korea expel its Russian representatives. As soon as Korea did so, though, Japanese companies bought land in Korea and built railroads from Seoul to Pusan to transport war materials for the anticipated battles with Russia. Little by little, the Japanese wedged their way into Korean affairs and forced the Korean emperor to hire a Japanese financial advisor, as well as advisors in police affairs, the ministry of defense, and the education ministry.

The Japanese came to use Incheon, located in modern-day northwestern South Korea, and other ports to launch naval attacks on Russian ships. In fact, Japan began to occupy much of Korea for its war preparations. Both sides engaged in bloody wars, mostly at sea. Even though they were victorious, the expense of the war nearly bankrupted Japan. Russia was in the throes of a revolution at home and was anxious to settle. In 1905, US President Theodore Roosevelt stepped in to mediate an end to the war and held the negotiations in Portsmouth, New Hampshire. However, in a secret discussion called the Taft-Katsura Memorandum, the United States agreed that Japan would keep its interests in Korea in exchange for Japan permitting the US to maintain its friendly relationship with the Philippines. It is not known for certain what happened during this meeting, as it was very secretive.

Once the Treaty of Portsmouth, the treaty that ended the Russo-Japanese War, was made public in 1905, Emperor Gojong and many of the Korean people staged protests. The Korean emperor said, "I declare that the so-called treaty of protectorate recently concluded between Korea and Japan was extorted at the point of the sword and under duress and therefore is null and void." In 1907, Gojong sent delegates to the Hague Peace Conference to protest the treaty, but his efforts were unsuccessful.

Prince Ito Hirobumi, who was made the Resident-General of Korea, proclaimed that the Korean emperor had acted against the treaty with his actions. As a result, Gojong was forced to abdicate his throne. Following that, his son, Sunjong, inherited the throne, but he was a minor and essentially powerless.

In 1910, a treaty of annexation was drawn up between Japan and Korea through the Resident-General, who handled Japan's role in Korea. Emperor Sunjong refused to sign it, so the prime minister of Korea, Ye Wanyong, did instead, raising questions about the legality of the document. However, despite these issues, Korea was annexed by Japan in 1910, dissolving the Korean Empire.

Government by Repression

After Korea had come so far in its efforts toward independence and more liberal attitudes that formed the basis for political parties, the Japanese overlords backstepped the country into a feudal-type status hierarchy. There was no free speech, and Korean representation wasn't allowed in the higher civil service positions. It was a militaristic-type of government; even the school teachers wore military uniforms and carried swords.

The Japanese plowed in and bought up as much land as they could because the Korean landowners couldn't pay the increased taxes that resulted from the expenses of the required irrigation, losing their lands that their families had spent so long trying to gain.

In 1912, the Governor-General, a position that overtook the Resident-General in late 1910 and was held by Terauchi Masatake at this time, had laws passed that essentially gave ownership of Korean land to the Japanese who were residing in Korea. The Koreans became tenant farmers and provided payments to the Japanese, leaving little for themselves. The Koreans were on the brink of starvation. Some of the farmers who weren't needed in Korea were assigned to go to mainland Japan and many of the South Pacific islands to work for Japan in construction, mining, and shipbuilding. In the same year, Japan created the "Regulations for Fisheries

Associations," which permitted not only Korean fishermen to work but Japanese fishermen as well. There were about 90,000 Japanese fishermen, and they depleted many of the fish that the Koreans had depended upon. In 1918, Japan passed the Korean Forestry Ordinance. Japanese lumber companies poured in and felled trees to provide lumber for Japan. The cleared land was then given to Japanese landowners to farm.

In terms of cultural identity, it was Japan's objective to "absorb" the Koreans into their way of life. According to a Japanese settler at the time, "The Korean people will be absorbed in the Japanese. They will talk our language, live our life, and be an integral part of us."

Within the next ten years, though, more liberalism was permitted, and political parties were able to form. The Koreans were even allowed to form labor unions and publish their own newspapers, but they were heavily censored.

Korean history books used in schools were edited to ensure that Japan was viewed in the most positive light possible. The histories were abridged in such a way as to eliminate any references to matters outside of the Korean Peninsula. Between 1910 and 1922, many private schools were closed, reducing the number from 2,000 to 600.

Japan was involved in World War I between 1914 to 1918 in an ancillary role. Korea wasn't directly involved, but Korean women and teenage girls were rounded up and forced to be "comfort women" for Japanese troops, in other words, sex slaves. Some of them were abducted from their homes, but most of them were lured by false promises of work or educational opportunities. A Korean survivor, Yun Doo Ri, stated this about her horrendous experience with a Japanese soldier, "He swiftly knocked me down and started pushing his thing inside me. It happened so fast. I found myself bleeding. I didn't know where the blood was coming from. I only felt pain. I was fifteen." These women and girls were badly mistreated, and later historians wrote that only a quarter of these girls survived.

In 1919, there was a huge Korean protest that demanded their independence. It was called the March 1st Movement, and although the demonstrations were peaceful, Japanese soldiers were called in to suppress the uprising. Around two million Koreans participated in the more than 1,500 demonstrations that took place throughout the country. Koreans believe that nearly 7,500 Koreans were killed, while Japanese officials at the time only reported 553 deaths; while it is not known for sure how many died, it is more than likely that several thousand did. Although many people died, the impetus for independence only grew among the Koreans.

Chapter 8 – Korea at War

Korea in World War II

In 1939, more than thirty countries were sucked into World War II, which started when Nazi Germany invaded Poland. When the Japanese attacked the US naval base at Pearl Harbor, Hawaii, in December 1941, America entered the war.

Japan had long craved mastery of the Pacific, along with its surrounding islands and the countries in Southeast Asia. The countries in the South Pacific afforded tremendous opportunities for trade and wealth. Elimination of most of the US Navy would have hindered the United States from engaging Japan in the Pacific theater. Japan had already annexed Manchuria, near the Chinese mainland, and installed a puppet government there. As part of their ambitions to expand the Japanese empire, they had allied themselves with the Axis powers of Germany and Italy in order to complete the conquest of China, along with the island kingdoms in the South Pacific.

Japan conscripted five million Koreans into their civilian war effort. Many of them were Japanese residents who had originally come from Korea during Japan's occupation of the country. They are called Zainichi Koreans, and, in fact, they comprise the second largest ethnic minority group in Japan today. These people worked in mines and factories that manufactured weapons and products for use by the Japanese soldiers on the front. The working conditions were deplorable, and as many as 60,000 of them died as a result.

About two percent of the Korean population was accepted from the 300,000 who voluntarily applied to join the Japanese Imperial Army. When Japan needed more soldiers in 1944, they inducted 200,000 more Korean men.

In early August 1945, the United States dropped atomic bombs on Nagasaki and Hiroshima. Although World War II had already ended in the European theater, this move ended the war in the Pacific one. The Allies, which included America, China, Great Britain, and the Soviet Union, among other countries, decided to strip Japan of all its conquests in the South Pacific, including Korea.

Before World War II officially ended, though, the Soviet Union invaded the Japanese puppet government in Manchuria, starting the Soviet-Japanese War a few days after the bombs were dropped on Japan. As a result of this war, the Soviet Union occupied the north of Korea, and the United States came in to occupy the southern part in September 1945, fearing Russian expansion. On September 12th, the People's Republic of Korea was established, which divided Korea into zones, with the Soviet Union in the north and the US in the south. The Soviet Union worked with the local People's Committee established there, passing sweeping reforms and redistributing the Japanese land to poor farmers. The old landed classes were not happy with this, and protests arose, with many fleeing south. The United States, on the other hand, refused to acknowledge the People's Republic of Korea, as it had communist elements in it, and outlawed it three months after its establishment. This led to people who supported the People's Republic to rise up; it is estimated that between 30,000 and 100,000 people were killed in the military campaigns against these insurgents over the course of a few years.

At the Moscow Conference in December 1945, it was agreed that the Soviet Union, the US, the Republic of China, and Great Britain would be a part of a trusteeship over Korea, which would end in five years when Korea would be declared independent and unified under one government. Although many Koreans wanted their independence, the trusteeship was put in place. A Soviet-US commission took place in 1946 and 1947 to work out the issues of a unified government but failed to make any progress. The Cold War tensions were already starting to seep in, and the Koreans were incredibly opposed to the trusteeship, making it hard to come to any conclusive agreements. As the commission bickered amongst themselves, the divisions between the two zones only deepened; in May 1946, it was illegal to cross the 38th parallel, the line that split the two zones, without a permit.

Since the commission wasn't making any progress, the issues were brought to the United Nations in 1947. The UN decided that Korea should elect a national assembly for the whole country and have the UN supervise the election. The Soviets rejected any form of election, and so, the elections were only held in the south. Koreans began to see this as the inevitable splitting up of their country, and protests against the elections began in 1948. However, the general election still took place in May. In August, the Republic of Korea took over the government from the US, with Syngman Rhee, an anti-communist and pro-American politician, as the president. In the north, the Democratic People's Republic of Korea was established in early September, with Kim Il-sung, a communist who had worked hard to get the Japanese out of his country, as the prime minister. Korea was officially split into two.

The Jeju Uprising

Jeju, a South Korean island, protested vehemently against the elections in 1947, a year before they even took place, as they knew it would lead to the splitting of Korea. The South Korean Labor Party (SKLP), or the Workers' Party of South Korea, a communist organization, led most of these protests, and as time went on, and as the election drew nearer, the protests became more frequent and more violent.

On April 3rd, 1948, 500 SKLP rebels, along with 3,000 other people who supported their cause, attacked the right-wing group Northwest Youth League, as well as police stations. Lieutenant General Kim Ik-ryeol attempted to solve the problem peacefully, but the two sides could not agree: the government wanted the rebels to completely surrender, while the rebels wanted the police to be disarmed, all government officials to be dismissed, the prohibition of paramilitary groups, and the reunification of the Korean Peninsula. The US sent forces to help squash the rebels, which worked for a time, as the rebels retreated. But at the end of April, the Korean governor of Jeju defected and joined the rebels, causing others in the military to do the same.

The fighting continued, picking up during the election week. The US feared that the rebels might be successful in stopping the elections from taking place and ordered a blockade of the island to prevent those sympathetic from the mainland in reaching Jeju. The rebels were not as active during the summer, but they picked back up once the elections in North Korea were about to take place, forming underground elections for those wanting to participate. The Republic of Korea (ROK) sent forces to help stop these activities, but they were unsuccessful, with one regiment deciding to assist the rebels once they arrived. ROK President Syngman Rhee was forced to declare martial law in mid-November, 1948. By the end of 1948, the ROK's harsh tactics had significantly damaged the rebel forces. They managed to launch one last offensive, but they were basically done.

Many civilians were killed during this uprising, most of them at the hands of the ROK and the US. It is thought that 14,373 civilians died, with some death tolls going as high as 30,000. The overall death toll goes up to as high as 100,000. About seventy percent of the island's villages were burned down, and recent discoveries have found mass graves of bodies.

This event was, for the most part, buried in history. For almost fifty years after the uprising, it was a crime for any South Korean to even mention the events of the Jeju uprising, punishable by beatings, torture, and/or a lengthy prison sentence. In the 1990s, though, the South Korean government openly admitted the atrocities that took place on the island, and in 2006, it issued an official apology.

The Korean War

When World War II ended, the Chinese Civil War resumed, which was between the government of the Republic of China, led by the Chinese Nationalist Party, and the Communist Party of China. In late September 1949, Mao Zedong established the People's Republic of China, and by August 1950, the Communist Party of China had won the war, placing Mao Zedong in charge.

Before that war fully ended, though, a new one had started. In March 1949, Kim Il-sung visited Joseph Stalin in Moscow and proposed a forcible reunification of Korea. Stalin agreed but wanted to wait to strike, as the time wasn't quite right. In the spring of 1950, Stalin believed the time was ripe; Mao Zedong had secured his final victory in China, and the US had withdrawn from Korea. Since the US didn't help in the Chinese Civil War, Stalin assumed they wouldn't come back to Korea to stop the spread of communist influence. As the Soviet Union had been supplying North Korea with arms, South Korea was becoming restless, knowing that war was imminent, and many clashes broke out along the 38th parallel.

On June 25th, 1950, the North Korean army crossed the 38th parallel and invaded South Korea. America, worried this could spread into another world war, wanted to move against North Korea, and they presented the issue to the United Nations. The United Nations condemned the invasion and decided to assist South Korea. The United Nations Command force (UNCOM) was placed under the leadership of US General Douglas MacArthur to expel the North Koreans and restore peace. The United States made up most of the force, but more countries volunteered to join the UN force or contribute in some way to the war effort.

First Battle of Seoul (June 25th to June 28th, 1950)

After North Korea crossed the 38th parallel, they marched toward Seoul. Using a blitzkrieg style of attacks, which the South Koreans could not stop, they easily took over the capital within three days. Seoul residents were advised to report on anyone who appeared to support South Korea and the UN. Former Korean newspapers were banned, and a photo of Kim Il-sung appeared on the front page of a newly published communist newspaper. The article in it blamed the war on Syngman Rhee, the South Korean president. It read, "Your bitter enemy is the traitor, Syngman Rhee, the tool of American imperialism."

Battle of Osan (July 5th)

At Osan, which is just south of the Korean capital of Seoul, a US task force moved in to repel the North Koreans. Unfortunately, the US force wasn't well equipped and only had 400 infantrymen, along with an artillery battery. The North Koreans, on the other hand, numbered to around 5,000 and had Soviet tanks to back them up. Although the US held them back, it was only temporary, and the North Koreans overran the Americans. This battle marked the first engagement between the US and North Korean forces.

Battle of Pyongtaek (July 6th)

The Americans retreated southward toward the city of Pyongtaek. They still didn't have the firepower they needed and regrouped there, as well as at Cheonan, also spelled as Chonan, which was farther south. Ammunition ran out, and communications equipment hadn't yet been sent in. In the face of the heavily armored Soviet-supplied T-34 tanks, the soldiers panicked and retreated in disorder.

Battle of Cheonan (July 7th to July 8th)

After receiving some ammunition and equipment, the US 34th Infantry Regiment and the 24th Infantry Division attempted to confront the North Koreans north of the town of Cheonan. The 3rd Battalion of the 34th Infantry set up a defensive perimeter on July 7th, and by nightfall, they were engaged with the North Koreans, who had moved in from the east and split into two columns. The 63rd Field Artillery unit, which was assisting the 34th Infantry, pelted the North Koreans and managed to hold off some of them.

It was at this point that the second column of the North Koreans arrived in the northwest, supported by the tanks. They destroyed motor vehicles in case any Americans were hiding in them. Colonel Robert Martin, the new commander of the 34th regiment, lost his life after being hit by tank fire. As the North Koreans kept pouring in, the troops up front were forced to retreat, and the back-up 1st Battalion withdrew under punishing mortar fire.

Battle of Chochiwon (July 10th to July 12th)

Forced to move even farther south, the newly assigned US 21st Infantry Regiment had orders to further delay the North Koreans in their southward advance until more men and equipment could be transported to South Korea. Much to the surprise of the American and UN forces, there were as many as 20,000 North Koreans but only 2,000 Americans and South Koreans to fight at Chochiwon. Airstrikes were carried on by US fighter planes called Mustangs, and they inflicted heavy damage on some of the powerful Soviet tanks.

The 1st Battalion, who had only held back-up positions at Cheonan, was now fully engaged with the North Koreans. The 3rd Battalion had a higher position on a ridge and regained some ground. They were also able to rescue some wounded men from the attacks that had occurred earlier in the day. The North Koreans had a multitude of machine guns and pommeled the UN positions heavily. Many of the infantrymen ran out of ammunition and had to engage in hand-to-hand combat. The UN troops lost 409 men, 140 were wounded, and 230 captured. Despite these losses, the 21st Infantry Regiment was praised for their work, as they managed to delay the North

Koreans long enough for the 24th Infantry Division to set up defenses around Taejon.

Battle of Taejon (July 14th to July 21st)

American soldiers from the 3rd Battalion and the 34th Infantry were fired upon by the North Koreans from across the Kum River, which ran west then turned south. They didn't hit the American infantry positions, as they were on higher ground. Soon, though, the North Koreans crossed the river and fired mortar rounds and artillery. Because they had very little communication equipment, the North Koreans were able to surround the American infantry. The 1st Battalion, which was farther north, also came under heavy attack, and it was able to hold off the North Koreans until the men could find safety. More North Koreans crossed the river, managing to capture an outpost of the 63rd Field Artillery Battalion. They managed to destroy communication lines and vehicles, as well as inflicted heavy losses, with the survivors retreating south on foot.

Where the river turned west, the American forces were joined by the 19th Infantry to shore up the 34th Infantry line, which brought anti-tank weapons, such as RPGs (rocket-propelled grenades) to the fighting front. Just then, the North Korean forces sent in large numbers of fresh troops against the 19th Infantry, who weren't able to hold them off. In the melee, the American supply lines were blocked off. The 2nd Battalion then moved in to break up the roadblocks that were set up to stop their supply lines. However, they suffered heavy casualties and were unable to do so.

Part of this fight at Taejon was actually intended to set up a defensive line to halt the North Korean advance, sending them back by controlling the Nakdong River that fed into the Kum. Thus, Brigadier General William Dean, the commander of the 24th Infantry, was ordered to hold the North Koreans back for as long as he could.

While Dean was defending that area, the North Koreans surrounded the city of Taejon, trapping the 24th and the 34th Infantry that were headquartered there. The North Koreans started occupying buildings, and there was intense house-to-house fighting for two days, with more North Koreans coming in, often disguised as farmers. Brigadier General Dean was there, as he had taken it upon himself to lead his men. He was captured, making him the highest-ranking prisoner during this war, but his identity wasn't known until much later.

Despite having fought bravely, the Americans were forced to withdraw once the North Koreans had the city nearly surrounded. Nearly 922 Americans were killed, 228 wounded, and 2,400 missing in action. It was later said by war historians that some of those soldiers who were missing or captured were immediately executed after the battle.

Although the battle was a loss for the Americans and South Koreans, it served the crucial purpose of buying time until their forces could set up a very strong defensive perimeter on the southeastern tip of South Korea, which included Pusan.

Battle of the Pusan Perimeter (August 4th to Sept 18th)

At this point in the war, Great Britain joined up with the UN forces. In the Battle of Taejon, the UN forces had to withdraw. However, a month later—in August—the UN was back to loosen North Korea's grip near the Kum River. This time, they focused on cutting the rail lines that were supplying the North Korean troops. Key railroad bridges were blown up, and more air attacks were inflicted upon them by the American bomber squadrons. The North Koreans lacked an adequate air defense, and at this point, many of their transport trucks had been destroyed. British ships, along with those of Australia, Canada, New Zealand, and the Netherlands, unloaded not only 600 tanks but also more men and weapons.

Task Force Pohang cleared the North Korean troops out of the mountainous regions, and Task Force Bradley waged ground battles to defend Pohang and invade the North Koreans at Anjang-ni. They engaged the North Koreans at the Nakong River, where they had been prior to the Battle of Taejon.

In August, troops in the Korean People's Army (KPA) was increased by forces fed in by North Korea. However, their supply lines didn't keep up with the pace, and they found themselves thinning out their lines to cover the whole perimeter. That was a weakness that could be exploited by the UN troops. The KPA was able to drive the UN forces southwest toward Masan, thus surprising them.

Securing control over the Nakdong River was essential in determining the outcome of this battle. In mid-August, General MacArthur initiated a carpet bombing of the KPA positions. This was somewhat effective because it reduced the number of North Korean forces trying to penetrate the south and broke their perimeter.

By late August, the paucity of supplies caught up with the KPA, along with the loss of their equipment. At that point, the UN ground forces outnumbered the North Koreans. Regardless, they concentrated their forces and broke the Pusan perimeter in some places. Fighting was intense at Haman, Kyongju, the Naktong Bulge (a segment of higher land near the river), Nam River, Jongsan, Taegu, and Kasan. This was known as the Great Naktong Offensive.

While the confrontations were being brutally fought in the Pusan regions, the UN carried out their stealthily laid plans to create an amphibious assault at Incheon called Operation Chromite. That offensive was going to move southeast to squeeze out the KPA contingents between there and Pusan. The KPA was caught by this deadly surprise and started retreating northward to escape the Pusan area.

This battle was one of the first crucial engagements in the war, and it raged for ten bloody days. As one soldier, Corp. Roy Alridge, worded it, "If we hadn't held the lines at Pusan, there would be no South Korea today."

Once most of the supply routes for the North Koreans had been cut off, and the KPA was facing increasing offensives from the UN troops, they began a humiliating retreat. The Battle of the Pusan Perimeter was a resounding victory for the UN troops.

Casualties were extreme at Pusan. The South Koreans had more than 40,000 casualties, while the North Koreans incurred almost 64,000.

Battle of Inchon (September 10th to September 19th)

The North Koreans were falling back from the Pusan perimeter, so a counterattack was planned by Douglas MacArthur to retake the area of Seoul. This operation was an amphibious assault at the southern city of Inchon, which involved around 75,00 troops and 261 ships. The decisive UN victory not only boosted morale, but it also allowed the UN forces to recapture Seoul about two weeks later. In this bold push north, the UN forces were able to resist the Chinese and North Korean troops and even got as far as the Yalu River, located on the border of North Korea and China.

The Armistice

By mid-December, the US was looking to discuss peace terms to end the war. South Korean President Syngman Rhee was in favor of unifying the entire Korean Peninsula under his command and did not want the peace talks to happen. Kim Il-sung also did not want to enter these talks, but he was pushed to enter into them by the People's Republic of China and the Soviet Union, whose help he would need to win the war anyway.

The peace talks began in June 1951, and they proceeded slowly. On July 27th, 1953, the Korean Armistice Agreement was signed. This was not a peace treaty but rather a ceasefire, so peaceful relations between the two countries were not set. The armistice established the Military Demarcation Line and the Korean Demilitarized Zone (DMZ). The DMZ was designed to be a buffer zone between the two nations and is 2.5 miles (4 kilometers) wide and 160 miles (250 kilometers) long. Troops from both sides guard the DMZ, and in 2018, it was the most heavily defended national border in the world.

Since there was no peace treaty, and since Syngman Rhee even refused to sign the agreement, the hostilities between the two nations still exist today.

Besides being known as the war that ultimately divided Korea, this war is also known for the numerous war crimes committed during it. In December of 1950, the South Korean president, Syngman Rhee, was furious about the fall of Pyongyang and executed communists and supporters of the opposition in what is known as the Bodo League massacre. It is estimated that at least 60,000 to 200,000 died. In July 1950, American servicemen killed an unknown number of South Korean refugees southeast of Seoul, believing them to be KPA soldiers. The South Korean side wasn't the only one to commit such atrocities, although they are better documented than the North Koreans. On June 28th, 1950, between 700 to 900 patients and medical staff were killed by the KPA in the Seoul National University Hospital massacre. The KPA has also been accused of beating, starving, and executing prisoners of war, although they deny such claims occurring on a widespread basis. One such massacre that they don't deny is the Hill 303 massacre, where 42 American prisoners of war were shot by the KPA, which led to KPA commanders enacting stricter guidelines on how to treat prisoners of war.

Chapter 9 – North Korea

Communism had undergone evolutionary changes during the 20th century and had split into Marxism-Leninism, Stalinism, Maoism (named after Mao Zedong of the People's Republic of China), and a flavor of communism promoted by Nikita Khrushchev when he was the premier of the Soviet Union from 1958 to 1964.

Stalin fostered a kind of "cult of personality" that Khrushchev abhorred. It promoted a kind of leader-worship, and Khrushchev preferred to return communism to the ideals of national collectivism and socialism. Stalin, on the other hand, flooded the country with self-portraits and controlled the press in such a way that it was his own personal mouthpiece. In his communique, "On the Cult of Personality and Its Consequences," Khrushchev called his process "de-Stalinization" and placed more authority in party leadership. Like Stalin, Kim Il-sung fervently believed in this cult approach. The history books published during his administration were revisionist, making it so that Kim's guerilla faction during World War II singlehandedly freed Korea from Japanese domination to impress upon North Korea his expertise in leadership.

When Kim Il-sung rose to power, there were four basic political factions: 1) the Pro-Soviet faction, who were Koreans who had lived in the Soviet Union since the 19th century; 2) the Domestic faction, which was composed of Koreans who did live in Korea but were vocally anti-Japanese, as many had been imprisoned by the Japanese during the occupation; 3) the Ya'an faction, who were Korean exiles who lived in China and joined the Communist Party of China; and 4) the Guerilla faction, who followed Kim Il-sung and who fought for the Soviet Army in Manchuria and later moved to the Soviet Union.

One by one, Kim eliminated his political rivals. In 1955, Pak Hon-yong, one of the main leaders of the communist movement in Korea, was arrested in a purge to rid North Korea of the members of the Workers' Party of Korea and was later executed. The real reason for his elimination, though, was his ability to attract huge numbers to his cause.

Three years later, Kim continued with his purge of potential rivals. In 1958, the leader of the Ya'an faction, Kim Tu-bong, mysteriously "disappeared." The leader of the Pro-Soviet faction was imprisoned in Pyongyang and murdered by the secret police in Korea in 1960. Members of the Pro-Soviet faction either joined Kim Il-sung's group or continue to live in the Soviet Union. Kim Il-sung merged the Workers' Party of Korea and the domestic faction.

Another noted individual, Li Sangjo, who was the Russian ambassador to North Korea, stated that the revolutionary struggle of the communist ideology was represented by Kim as being his own personal efforts to overthrow the Japanese overlords and that he exaggerated his own role in "liberating Korea." His campaign was dominated by presenting himself as "wise," a "genius," and an "iron commander."

Kim had absolute power in the country. North Korea, to this day, promotes self-reliance, or *Juche*, as a state ideal, indicating that North Korea is self-sufficient and truly independent. The *Juche* concept promotes economic sustainability through its own agriculture, and as a result, Kim isolated North Korea from the rest of the world.

The Songbun System

In 1958, Kim divided the population into three categories: 1) the core class, who were considered faithful followers of the regime; 2) the wavering class, who were perceived as being ambivalent toward Kim and his party's ideals; and 3) the hostile class, those who were openly hostile or had the potential to be hostile toward the North Korean government. The core class consisted of laborers in agriculture or factories, as well as high-ranking people who served in government posts. The wavering group was comprised of the ordinary Koreans who did not care much about politics or were uninformed. The hostile group consisted of former landowners and subversives, as they were the most likely to rebel against Kim Il-sung and the government. Files were kept on everyone and even included family backgrounds. With the exception of the core class, suspicion continued to be associated with those perceived as wavering or hostile, regardless of their future actions.

Agriculture in North Korea

Juche is at the center of agriculture in North Korea. A public distribution system was established in the 1950s, which required that farmers hand over seventy percent of their produce to the government for distribution to urban areas that could not grow food products. However, only seventeen percent of the land in North Korea can be farmed, as most of the nation is mountainous. The high elevations are rocky and uneven, which is unsuitable for farming, although some cattle grazing is possible at the lower elevations. The warm season is only three months long, and it is very rainy. Thus, there is the potential for flooding that can ruin crops. The flooding does, however, favor rice paddy farming if constructed on slopes and terraces. This is only possible in the southern areas of North Korea, though, as it is too cold farther north to do that. A lot of farmers fled the land in search of manufacturing, a low-level government or civil service job, or signed up for a career in the military. Many farmers and their families starved.

Farmers today work on state-run farms and collective farms, which are huge tracts of land cultivated by large groups of farmers. Unfortunately, it suffers from natural disasters, like floods and periods of droughts. The foodstuffs are then transported to the city areas and distributed there. Many of the crops are diverted for consumption by the elite and the military first and then to the factory workers and others in the urban areas.

Those who own some land around their homes often raise their own vegetable gardens for their families and neighbors. Mechanization is sparse, as are repairs and lack of spare parts, making farming a labor-intensive process. Fertilizers and biochemical elements that would enhance crop production is severely lacking but has improved over the years. The distribution system intended for a whole country is logistically very cumbersome, and there are significant delays in getting food to markets; thus, food is subsequently rationed.

In the 1990s, some mechanisms were introduced, and an irrigation system was put into place in the more arid areas. Rain and rice are more easily grown in North Korea now, but there is a lack of protein due to the lower intake of animal products, eggs, and beans. Protein deficiency is extremely severe, resulting in muscular weakness and even fluid buildup and edema. The areas of arable land are conducive to growing rice, potatoes, soybeans, sugar beets, mulberry, sorghum wheat, barley, and millet.

Food shortages are common in North Korea. The World Food Program estimates six million tons of grain are needed to feed the population, but only three million tons of grain are produced. In the mid-1990s, North Korea had huge food shortages. Between 1992 and 1998, it was estimated that nearly three million people died of starvation. In 2006, the production of wheat and barley decreased by nearly eighty percent, causing famine. This shortage was due to soil depletion and the fact that many farmers opted to work in the cities if they could.

The decline of the economy in North Korea is progressively getting worse. In 2014, North Korea passed the Enterprise Act, which permitted some foreign trade and joint ventures with other countries. Dr. Mitsuhiro Mimura, a Japanese research consultant, visited North Korea on numerous occasions and has called it the "poorest advanced economy in the world." Most of their money is devoted to nuclear development and defense instead of agricultural advancements.

Industrialization

North Korea operates on the principles of a "command economy," which means that the government determines what products are made, the quantity that needs to be made, and the prices that are charged for the goods. Following the Korean War, North Korea emphasized heavy industry. Tractors, bulldozers, and generators were manufactured and exported to the Middle East rather than being used for North Korea. Infrastructure and poor delivery system slowed the progress and movement of equipment and supplies.

North Korea has no oil or gas of its own. It does have anthracite coal, which is the hardest form of coal. That calls for the construction of mines and requires the construction of heavy-duty equipment to extract the coal from the earth and even more to transform it into acceptable fuel. They imported Western-style machinery and adopted some of the up-to-date management styles of those countries, including China, the Soviet Union, and even South Korea. Transportation systems were upgraded, along with automation. Education was expanded to train technicians and specialists in the fields of fuel, electronic, mechanical, and automation engineering.

By the 1970s, North Korea went into debt. The failure to maintain the equipment plus the lack of skills to do so shut down some factories. Because most of its money is spent on defense and the military, the economy stagnated. Estimates indicate that as much as forty percent of its revenue is spent on the manufacture of weapons. In 1993, North Korea established the Rason Special Economic Zone, which promoted foreign investment. There was some improvement in sales and income, but their structures are still undeveloped. Most of their trade is with China, which accounts for ninety percent of their imports. The per capita income of North Korea is only 1,700 US dollars.

Economic assistance came from China and the Soviet Union, but the Soviet Union started to demand hard currency for its imports, including oil. In the 1990s, China also reduced its imports. After the split of the Soviet Union in 1991, imports from them also decreased. Along with natural disasters, such as floods and droughts, North Korea was forced into an economic crisis.

By 1993, the North Koreans announced that it had completed a light-water nuclear reactor, capable of producing ten million kWh (kilowatt hour) of electricity annually. They then experimented with the light-water reactor to enrich uranium, which is needed for bringing it up to weapons-grade status. The process is slow, but a gas centrifuge is more efficient. There have been no reports of gas centrifuges in North Korea, though. The International Atomic Energy Agency wanted to inspect their facilities, specifically the Nyongbyon Nuclear Scientific Research Center, but Kim Il-sung declined. Pakistan, who possesses nuclear weapons, admitted in 2005 that they sold some nuclear technology to North Korea during the 1970s that could be used to manufacture nuclear weapons.

Lack of Electricity

In 1990, North Korea had some electricity, which was fueled by coal, oil, and hydroelectric plants. As political conditions changed in China and Russia, their electrical output severely decreased. The North Koreans use solar panels to generate what electricity they can, but overcast and rainy days decrease the yield of those panels. Satellite photos taken at night reveal the paucity of electricity. The

Korean Peninsula shows South Korea and China well-lit at night, but North Korea is almost totally dark.

Nuclear Armament

The armistice forbade the proliferation of nuclear weapons in either North Korea or South Korea. The United States made a statement shortly after the armistice that it wouldn't necessarily abide by the paragraph banning nuclear weapons. Between 1958 and 1991, the US stored nuclear weapons in South Korea.

South Korea again considered building new nuclear missiles and conducted a test. After revisiting the issue, South Korea decided against it. In 1968, South Korea and North Korea signed the Treaty on the Non-Proliferation of Nuclear Weapons. The US removed its nuclear weapons from the Korean Peninsula, but in 2003, North Korea withdrew from the non-proliferation agreement and have since started conducting nuclear tests.

In 2006, North Korea announced that it launched its first successful nuclear test underground. The explosion was confirmed by seismic readings taken in the West. The West vehemently reacted, but North Korea, who desperately needed oil shipments that had embargoes placed on it, indicated it was willing to shut down its nuclear research station at Nyongbyon. Meetings were conducted between North Korea, South Korea, China, Japan, Russia, and the United States. However, the talks were suspended when North Korea conducted another nuclear test in 2009.

In 2011, Kim Jong-il died of a suspected heart attack, and his death was followed by an elaborate funeral. Psychologists have labeled him as paranoid, anti-social, and narcissistic. He was later called the "Shining Star," and his body is preserved and displayed at Pyongyang's Kumsusan Memorial Palace. He was succeeded by his son, Kim Jong-un, who has carried on his policies.

In 2010, North Korea experimented with a different type of nuclear reaction. The traditional nuclear reaction is that of nuclear fission, where an atom is split by the bombardment of high-energy neutrons (non-charged) particles. This sets off a chain reaction, and the radioactive fallout is immense, like that which occurred at Nagasaki and Hiroshima during World War II. Fusion is another type of manipulation of the atom in which lighter atoms are combined. This produces a tremendous amount of energy and is similar to the kind of nuclear reactions in the sun. The reaction is huge, more so than that of an atomic bomb, although it produces far less radioactivity. Hydrogen bombs use the hydrogen atom for fusion. Experts who analyzed the purported fallout, though, doubt that the test was the result of fusion.

In 2012, under Kim Jong-un, North Korea agreed to suspend their uranium enrichment programs and was slated to receive food aid from the United States as an incentive. However, later that same year, North Korea armed a nuclear warhead on an antiballistic missile and tested it. In response, those food aid packages were canceled.

In 2017, China announced that it would suspend all oil shipments to North Korea—a fuel that they had used to generate electricity and create gasoline for the few cars it had manufactured. Shortly after this, North Korea launched four ballistic missiles, which landed in the Sea of Japan. Later the same year, North Korea launched two more, but they exploded shortly after they were launched. By the end of that year, North Korea was successful and claims that it now has the capability of launching a missile that could hit the United States mainland.

In 2003, six nations—China, Japan, the United States, Russia, North Korea, and South Korea—met to resolve the nuclear issue. No agreement has yet been formulated, but a framework for discussions has been laid out. They met again in 2009, but nothing was resolved. In 2018, Kim Jong-un announced that he was committed to the denuclearization of the Korean Peninsula.

As of 2019, the Bulletin of Atomic Scientists, a nonprofit organization concerned about global security issues, estimates that

North Korea has between twenty and thirty nuclear weapons. In October the same year, Kim Jong-un, US President Donald Trump, and South Korean President Moon Jae-in held several meetings about the nuclear issue and the final resolution of the Korean War, but no agreement has been forthcoming yet.

Biological and Chemical Weapons

North Korea signed the Geneva Protocol, a treaty that prohibits the use of chemical and biological weapons in international fights, in 1989. However, North Korea never signed the Chemical Weapons Convention, which means it has no obligation to refrain from producing or stockpiling chemical weapons. Intelligence sources indicate that it possesses biological agents that can be easily combined to create a weaponized version of anthrax and smallpox, and reports also indicate that it has stockpiled mustard gas, phosgene, sarin, and V-type chemical agents. V-type agents cause its victims to lose muscular control, making them subject to seizures, uncontrollable urination, vomiting, and foaming at the mouth. Phosgene intoxicates the lungs, making its victims choke to the point that they are unable to breathe.

The Rulers

Kim Il-sung was the first premier of North Korea and ruled from 1948 to 1972. After 1972, his title was changed to president, and he remained in power until his death in 1994. Having been in the military most of his earlier adult life, Il-sung styled his country that way. It was austere and highly regimented. To wield his power, Il-sung remained as the head of the Korean Workers' Party for his lifetime and virtually made others join it. Although he upheld the principle of "self-reliance" and preferred isolationism, the country lacked the natural resources to supply all the food and oil it needed. So, it became necessary to open up trade relations with other countries, but Il-sung restricted the number of those countries. In 1994, he signed the Agreed Framework, an agreement with the

United States in which North Korea would refrain from producing nuclear weapons in exchange for an outside firm that would build two light-water nuclear reactors for the production of electricity. In 1983, North Korea attempted to assassinate President Chun Doo-hwan of South Korea and bombed Flight 858 to Seoul from Iraq, causing the United States and other countries to impose sanctions on North Korea.

Kim Il-sung was succeeded by his son, Kim Jong-il. Kim Jong-il didn't assume the title of president because that was reserved for the first president, his father, who is referred to as the "Eternal President." Therefore, Jong-il became the chairman of the National Defense Commission. His goal was a warming of relations between the two Koreas, and he met with South Korean President Kim Dae-jung to discuss those possibilities. In 1999, the United States agreed to lift some of the sanctions against the country in exchange for ceasing to test a long-range missile. By outward appearances, it seemed that Jong-il was abiding by the Agreed Framework his father had signed, but high-level intelligence reports indicated otherwise. In 2003, Jong-il announced the detonation of an underground nuclear weapons test. The US and North Korea attempted to write another agreement and came up with one in 2007, but it was left in abeyance over the issue of compliance. In 2011, Kim Il-sung died, and he was succeeded by his son, Kim Jong-un.

Kim Jong-un, like his grandfather, utilized the practice of eliminating his rivals or those within his administration who displeased him. When Kim Jong-un took power, his uncle, Jang Song-thaek, had been serving as a director of the Youth Work Department within the Workers' Party of Korea (WPK) Central Committee. He later became a member of the WPK Central Committee and was spoken about as if he might be the next successor of North Korea after Kim Jong-il.

Song-thaek was seen again in March 2006 and later became the vice-director of the WPK and the vice-commissioner of the National Defense Commission. In 2013, he promulgated the construction of a bridge over the Yalu River but was glaringly absent at the dedication ceremony. Rumors from observers indicated that Kim Jong-un was displeased by what he perceived as cordial relations being discussed with China by Song-thaek. Then a dispute over control of the fishing rights between the Chinese and Korean fishermen occurred, which Song-thaek ultimately couldn't control. In addition, defectors to South Korea said that Song-thaek drank heavily at times and more than once made comments about North Koreans dying of hunger. In 2013, Kim Jong-un had his uncle arrested. He was tried by a special military tribunal and sentenced to execution. Song-thaek was dragged out into a yard and killed by antiaircraft machine guns, after which his body was burnt. Two of his deputies, Ri Ryong-ha and Jang Su-gil, were also slaughtered in the same fashion.

Many other influential members of the North Korean government have been killed in recent years. In 2014, O Song-hon, who worked for Jang Song-thaek, had followed his orders to create a separate arm for security for business purposes. He was executed by firing squad. A co-worker, Pak Chu-hong, was also executed. In 2015, Choe Yong-gon, one of the vice-premiers of North Korea and the deputy minister of construction and building, was reportedly executed after having got into an argument with Kim Jong-un over an issue related to forestry; he actually disappeared from public life, so it is unknown what happened to him. In 2016, Kim Jong-un's top educational official, Kim Jong-jin, was executed by a firing squad for being branded as an "anti-party and a counter-revolutionary" for showing a bad attitude during a meeting of the National Assembly.

Human Rights in North Korea

Freedom of speech is restricted, and the criticism of the government is forbidden. If one speaks out against the government or its leaders, they are sent to reeducation camps. Television, radio, and publishing are controlled by the government, as the praise and promotion of the country's supreme leader comes first before all else. Films and plays all circulate around the cult of personality, and criticism of the United States and other capitalistic countries appears in government-censored newspapers. Broadcasts from South Korea are also prohibited. North Korea uses a different coding system for broadcasting than South Korea, so it isn't even possible to view South Korean television programs in North Korea. Tampering with signals is a serious offense and results in a criminal penalty.

The practice of religion isn't technically forbidden, but there is no true freedom of religion in the country, as Christians, in particular, are targeted by the country. It is said that the Christians in North Korea are the most persecuted in the world. Christianity, as well as other religions, is practiced in secret. The only religions that are somewhat accepted are Buddhism and Confucianism.

All charity organizations and non-governmental organizations are carefully scrutinized. Anyone found to be proselytizing or practicing religions is imprisoned and subjected to harsh treatment. Estimates of religious prisoners are around 60,000 people. Some Buddhist temples remain but are mainly viewed as a part of the history of the country and do not actively engage in religious worship or practices. There are five churches in Pyongyang—three Protestant, one Russian Orthodox, and one Catholic. They are there for foreigners and for propaganda purposes.

Travel is severely restricted, and views of the cities from above show neatly laid-out but empty streets. Fuel is in low supply, and only the elite own vehicles. The people aren't permitted to relocate or move freely around the country, although people have managed to flee the country. Those who are forced back to Korea are often beaten and sent to prison camps, as they are deemed as defectors. Immigration and emigration are curtailed, and anyone returning from China, in particular, are punished.

Chapter 10 – South Korea

Just like any country, South Korea's history isn't picture-perfect. In 1949, just prior to the outbreak of the Korean War, several divisions of the South Korean army massacred unarmed civilians in the North Gyeongsang Province of South Korea, which is located on the eastern shore. The victims included women, children, and the people, all of whom were accused of being communist sympathizers. The South Korean government under Syngman Rhee, the newly elected president of South Korea, blamed Kim Il-sung's guerilla faction for being responsible. That wasn't the case, though. Many years later, South Korea admitted their involvement in the massacre, which resulted in the deaths of 75 people.

Rocky Beginnings

In 1948, Syngman Rhee was elected as president of the First Republic of Korea. Despite its announced commitment to democracy, Rhee was autocratic. He was also accused of corruption and of killing his political opponents. When he was elected for his fourth term in 1956, students in the port city of Masan rebelled, claiming the elections were rigged. Students staged an enormous revolt, which spread to the capital city of Seoul, and when the body of a student was found floating in the river along with 186 bodies, they were incensed. Martial law was then imposed, and Rhee resigned, fleeing to Hawaii to live in exile.

In 1960, Yun Posun was elected as president to the Second Republic of Korea, as the massive protests had established a new parliamentary government. Posun was more of a figurehead than anything else, as the real power was with the prime minister. Neither man could gain loyalty from any of the major political parties, leaving the government in a tough spot, especially since the economy was suffering due to the corruption of the prior government. Major General Park Chung-hee formed the Military Revolutionary Committee, aiming to overthrow the government. In May 1961, he staged a coup, overthrowing the government of Yun Posun and putting a military government in its place. This began the Third Republic of South Korea, which was, in practice, a dictatorship. It was ruled by the Democratic Republican Party and the Supreme Council, as well as Park Chung-hee, although Yun Posun remained president until 1962.

In 1963, Park was elected as president by a slim margin over Yun Posun, and in 1967, he was reelected for another term. The National Assembly, who, for the most part, favored Park, passed an extraordinary amendment allowing Park to run for a third term. He ran against Kim Dae-jung and won, again by a slim majority. In 1971, Park declared a state of emergency. He indicated that it was because of the "dangerous realities of the international situation," but more likely, it was an effort to reorganize the government in such a way that he could assume some form of dictatorial control over the country.

During this period of time, Park met with Kim Il-sung of North Korea to discuss the reunification of Korea. In anticipation of that, he called for revitalization reforms, starting with the forming of a conference consisting of around 2,500 elected members who would serve for six years. He announced the inauguration of the Yushin Constitution, but it was merely intended to give Park dictatorial powers. In 1972, after the passing of the constitution, the Fourth Republic of Korea was founded, granting him the powers he wanted. The Yushin Constitution forbade any opposition to the Yushin declaration itself and permitted Park to arrest anyone who opposed it. It also exempted low-income people from taxes and banned the known student protestor organizations and closed their schools.

In 1973, Park's former presidential opponent, Kim Dae-jung, was kidnapped from where he had been living in Japan and taken to Seoul. It was felt by those in power that this was triggered by his criticism of Park Chung-hee's attempts to seize dictatorial powers. Dae-jung's followers feared for his welfare, and the opposition against Park continued to grow among the people until it escalated into a major crisis.

In 1975, a large opposition group, who was trying to revive the People's Revolutionary Party, was arrested by the Korean Central Intelligence Service. They were accused of trying to set up a socialist state. One thousand twenty-four individuals were arrested, without warrants, and 253 of them were imprisoned. Less than five days later, eight of the leaders were sentenced to death, and eighteen hours later, they were executed.

In October 1979, Park himself was assassinated by the head of the Korean Central Intelligence Service. Martial law was declared the next day, and Choi Kyu-hah, the prime minister, stepped in as acting president and was officially elected as president in December. A coup was led shortly after by Major General Chun Doo-hwan, and by early 1980, the rebels basically controlled the government. Choi was made the head of the Korean Central Intelligence Agency in April 1980, and by May, he had dropped all pretense of not being the leader and declared martial law. Protests erupted, and the country was in chaos.

Gwangju Uprising

When martial law was declared by Chun Doo-hwan, universities were shut down. Around 200 angry students collected at the gates of Chonnam National University on May 18th, 1980. Suddenly, a unit of paratroopers arrived to disperse the crowd. The mob then moved down the main street and continued to grow until the crowd accumulated an estimated number of 2,000 protestors. More and more soldiers were sent in, and the episode erupted into violence. Troops beat demonstrators and even fired upon them. The protest spread not only to students but also to the general populace, which objected to the stringency of the new administration. Buses arrived loaded with demonstrators, and people flooded the streets. Citizens even seized arms from police stations and armories. A negotiation committee consisting of clergymen, lawyers, and professors reorganized the massive crowd into two groups, the Student Settlement Committee and the Citizens Settlement Committee. However, these groups were unable to make any progress in negotiating with the army.

The protest then spread to other provinces, such as Naju, Hwasan, Haenam, Mokpo, Yeongam, Muan, and Gangjin. Army forces were then sent to quell the insurrection in those sectors. On May 27th, after nine days of heavy fighting and protesting, the rebellion was suppressed in Gwangju. There is no universally accepted number of the dead for this tragic incident. The official figures released by the government stated that the death toll for the civilian population was a little less than 150. However, it has been argued that the death toll was closer to 1,000 or even 2,000.

Chun Doo-hwan Becomes President

After the intelligence chief, Choi, resigned in August, Chun Doo-hwan was recognized officially as president. In March 1981, the name of the government had changed once more, becoming the Fifth Republic of South Korea, which was a dictatorship and a one-party state under the Democratic Justice Party. Despite all of this political chaos, the economy expanded, and Chun altered Park's system of keeping economic decision-making in the top levels of government. Instead, he felt that economic decision-making should rely upon experts who were familiar with the market. An Economic Planning Board was established, although a lot of the traditionalists resented surrendering control. Because of that infighting, in fact, Dow Chemical, who had plants in South Korea, left the country. IBM had also considered investments in South Korea, but the political turmoil caused them to decide against it. Due to the pressure from conservative groups, Chun maintained a strong governmental presence in working with businesses but did insist upon American and European consultants in South Korea to aid in economic development.

In 1982, the Planning Board developed a five-year plan for expansion and hired a think tank, which had significant input from foreign business experts. Due to Chun's efforts to bridge the gap between the traditional and the liberal approaches to handling international business affairs, compromises were reached. In a CIA report released in 2018 about South Korea's economy in 1982, the conclusion was positive: "We believe the overall efficiency of South Korea's economic decision-making structure and the policies in place will enable the country to achieve a fairly good growth rate in the coming year." According to the Institute for International Economics, South Korea experienced what is called a "miracle economy."

Leading to Free Elections

Over time, the Fifth Republic slowly turned into a democratic state. In 1987, Chun Doo-hwan declared Roh Tae-woo to be the Democratic Justice Party, which effectively handed the role of president to him. Massive protests occurred throughout the country due to this, and Roh promised that a direct presidential election would occur, as well as a more democratic constitution. Chun resigned as the head of the party in July 1987, and the first honest election that South Korea had seen in twenty years took place in December, with Roh Tae-woo winning. This established the Sixth Republic of Korea, the current government in place.

Exploding Economy

Since the 1960s, South Korea expanded exponentially with some notable exceptions during financial downturns. Industries were initially springboarded by huge family-owned conglomerates like

Hyundai and Samsung. Because of their potential financial resources, they were given tax incentives and interest-free financing. Workers' wages steadily increased, and their work conditions improved. South Korea's gross national product doubled in thirty years' time.

Because the country lacks a lot of natural resources, it mostly depends on exports. Foreign investment was greatly encouraged due to the low rate of personal savings. Industries and businesses were not only encouraged to update frequently, but they also had to in order to compete in the global market.

One of their largest businesses, even today, is the Hyundai Corporation. The founder, Chung Ju-yung, started the business as a repair garage during the Japanese occupation of Korea. Once it was replaced with a steel mill, he was forced out of business but had managed to save some money. After Korea was freed from Japanese control, he took advantage of foreign investments to establish the Hyundai Civil Industries Corporation in conjunction with American engineers. After the Korean War, the company helped reconstruct the country. Chung Ju-yung contributed his organizational skills, and his physical ones as well, into helping to construct the Soyang Dam in 1967, the Gyeongbu Expressway in 1968, and the Kori Nuclear Power Plant in 1972. In 1975, using consultants from Europe, he introduced his first car, the Hyundai Pony, following it up with the Hyundai Excel in 1986, a vehicle still sold today. In the 1990s, Hyundai had acquired eight financial affiliates.

In 1984, measures were adopted by the South Korean government that permitted Samsung to expand into the insurance market. In 1988, when Roh Tae-woo was the South Korean president, it initiated a credit card company and later purchased a securities firm. In the 1990s, also under Roh's administration, Samsung became one of the largest non-bank financial companies in the country.

A large competitor in the financial investment market was LG Corporation. It created Goldstar Investment in 1982, Konghae Mutual Savings Bank in 1985, and LG Investment Trust in 1988.

Loans were readily available to the larger companies, so Samsung, LG Corporation, and Hyundai all participated in the semiconductor industry during Roh's administration. Samsung had already done so years earlier, but the quality of their equipment wasn't up to par by comparison until they learned more about the industry.

Semiconductor Industry

While Park was still in office, Korea developed its own digital switching system, the TDX-1, and the government made it a proprietary product through its own research and development program, the Electronics and Telecommunications Research Institute (ETRI). The digital switching system is used for the construction of telecommunications networks. Under the administration of Roh Tae-woo and his successor, Kim Young-sam, the industry created the VLSIC (very large-scale interface circuit chips) in conjunction with the ETRI, called the ETRI-VSIC. Samsung, as well as smaller private manufacturers, added a fiber-optic cable to that system and thus secured a large portion of the global market once the business arm of Roh Tae-woo's and Kim Young-sam's governmental bodies liberalized trade policies and could license products across the world. Once they were freed from government constraints, Samsung, Goldstar, and Daewoo Electronics could market these products to the world. Their competitors on the world stage were AT&T, GED, and IBM. South Korea had truly proven itself as an accomplished first-world company.

In 1988, South Korea made a monumental advance in the semiconductor industry by adapting dynamic random-access memory (DRAM) to their TDX-1, making it compatible with their digital switching system. That technology wasn't unique to the South Koreans, but they were the first to make it adaptable.

The South Korean government had its hand in all these technological developments, unlike other countries with purely free enterprise. It was a benefit to South Korea, as they needed government-sponsored funding; however, that brought with it the problems of government regulations.

Non-Telecommunication Industrial Development

Besides the telecommunications industry, South Korea partakes in shipbuilding. The usual conglomerates were the first to enter the field: Hyundai Heavy Industries, Daewoo Shipbuilding and Marine Engineering, and Samsung Heavy Industries. Mining is a much smaller but important industry in South Korea because it can supply the prized minerals—tungsten, graphite, coal, and molybdenum, a silvery metal with a high melting point that is useful in the manufacture of metal alloys.

The Korea Railroad Corporation, Korail, is a high-speed railway system that is far improved from its ancestor, the Korean National Railroad, which was founded in 1963. In 2005, it split into the Korea Rail Network Authority and Korail. The railways are a complex network that operates intercity, commuter, and freight trains.

Obstacles to Trade Overcome

The government under Chun Doo-hwan, as well as the prior presidents, had a heavy hand in creating protectionist barriers to open trade. In the telecommunications market, in particular, South Korea was very slow to remove those barriers, many of which had to do with the regulations that they had to use their own inspection teams.

From 1998 to 2003, South Korean President Kim Dae-jung emphasized the economy above all else. The growth rate was ten percent in 1999 and 9.2 percent the following year. The bigger companies were restructured to curtail monopolies, leaving more opportunities for other developers. Some free trade agreements were signed under Kim Dae-jung, including the Korea-Australia Free Trade Agreement.

During the recession period of 2008 to 2009, South Korea had a downturn, but so did the rest of the world. After some bankrupt industries left the market, South Korea was still able to recover.

Korea also underwent a financial crisis in 1997, but its fame as a well-developed industrial country aided in them being able to obtain a loan from the International Monetary Fund. This economic shake-up led to the loss of Kim Young-sam's reelection bid and the subsequent election of Kim Dae-jung in 1998. Kim Dae-jung received the Nobel Peace Prize in 2000 for his Sunshine Policy, which emphasized communication with North Korea, as North Korea was facing bankruptcy and starvation at the time. Kim Dae-jung is the only Korean to have won a Nobel Prize so far.

The Korean Wave

In the 21st century, South Korea became a major exporter of popular culture, giving rise to what is called the Korean Wave, which started its incline in the 1990s. The government of South Korea provides subsidies to its art and music, not only for the sake of entertainment but to publicize itself as an independent country. In 1999, South Korea's first big-budget film, *Shiri*, became a blockbuster and even surpassed the box-office record of *Titanic* in South Korea.

In 1999, K-pop music became incredibly popular on the internet, mostly via YouTube. In 2016, eighty percent of music videos circulated throughout the East were made in Korea and featured Korean artists. Outside of Asia, the United States became one of the largest consumers for K-pop music. Elements of Chinese and Japanese influences are present in this music, but it is a style unique to Korea.

The Korean Wave washed over China as well. In 2000, the Korean boy band H.O.T. (Highfive of Teenagers) was being sold out in China along with Super Junior. One of the most successful K-pop groups of 2016 was Big Bang, which was recorded to have earned nearly $44 million.

Korean romance dramas are shown across East Asia, including Nepal and Sri Lanka. In India, Korean films were forbidden, but they were squirreled in via the black market. This rage among the youth just could not be halted.

Korean restaurants became popular in other countries as well. Kimchi, a traditional Korean dish, was even served at the White House under US President Barack Obama. Korea has also bought numerous resorts in the United States and has some of the finest golf courses in the country.

Chinese consumers buy billions of dollars of Korean-manufactured cosmetics and skincare products. Korea has beauty products carefully constructed to suit the various shades of Asian skin, making it highly desirable.

Political Situation in the 21st Century

President Lee Myung-bak of South Korea met with President George W. Bush in 2008. Among the issues they discussed were solutions for the global recession that occurred during that time, as well as diplomatic relations. In their discussions, Lee and Bush had agreed to lift the ban on beef imports due to unfounded fears of "mad cow disease."

There were also controversies within the Cabinet, which Lee remedied by reshuffling his Cabinet officials and implementing industrial and administrative reforms. South Korea then reached out to the world by holding a summit in Seoul with other Asian countries.

Park Geun-hye served as president from 2013 to 2017. She was the first female president of the country, as well as the first president to be born after South Korea had been officially founded. After a series of scandals involving her and her administration came to light, she was impeached, and Prime Minister Hwang Kyo-ahn stepped in as acting president. Although his term of service was short, he focused upon security against North Korea at the Northern Limit Line, which clarifies the maritime border in the Yellow Sea between North Korea and South Korea, to prevent any incidents. After his tenure as acting president, Hwang Kyo-ahn joined the Liberty Korea Party, becoming the president of the party in early 2019. He opposes the Sunshine Policy, which helps to warm the relationships with North Korea and is seeing a revival under the current South Korean president, Moon Jae-in.

He was elected in 2017, and besides favoring the Sunshine Policy, he supports a proposal to build a natural gas pipeline that would originate in Russia and go through North Korea as well as South Korea. However, he is very concerned about North Korea's recent launches of intercontinental ballistic missiles. Prior to his election, Moon was opposed to a proposition with the United States for the use of the THAAD, the Terminal High Altitude Area Defense system, which was designed to destroy any incoming missiles. However, he changed his mind after the election and made an agreement with the US to set up a temporary system for South Korea's defense. His goal is the eventual reunification of North and South Korea and the non-proliferation of nuclear weapons. Moon and Kim have had two confidential meetings about reunification to date.

Although he is pro-American, Moon Jae-in has presented some reservations. "I'm pro-US, but now South Korea should adopt diplomacy in which it can discuss a request and say 'No' to Americans." He still recognizes the US as friends but wants to be sure that South Korea takes the lead.

Conclusion

Korea began as a humble little peninsula jutting into the Yellow Sea. They were home to many clans at the beginning, which brought about bloody rivalries that were only tempered by a hard-working population of independent and free-thinking people who wanted freedom from the grand and overwhelming dynasties of China. Although forced to seek the aid of such dynasties at times, the Koreans were very selective in terms of whom they chose to interact with. Trade was their initial goal, as well as freedom from the raging nomadic tribes seeking to overtake what was most precious to them—their farms and their unique cultures. They were practical people committed to survival who rejected intrusion by those who wanted to assimilate them into a people of their own making. Having been subjects to raids from other nomadic groups and aggressive nations in the Pacific, they took what they felt was valuable from those other cultures and rejected that which didn't suit their Buddhist and Confucian beliefs.

Koreans excel in intelligence and innovation, and South Korea is the third-largest economic force in the Pacific region after China and Japan today. They became isolated for a time but eventually compromised to accept help from other industrial nations without permitting themselves to become imitators of such cultures.

Currently, Kim Jong-un of North Korea and Moon Jae-in of South Korea are making overtures toward the reunification of the split country. In 2018, South Korea hosted the Winter Olympics, in which North Korea took part. In addition, separated families from both sides have had several reunion events, where they were able to socialize with members they might not have ever even met before. South Korean President Moon Jae-in has proposed that 2045 might be the year that the two portions of the country will be unified once again.

Here are some other books by Captivating History that we think you would find interesting

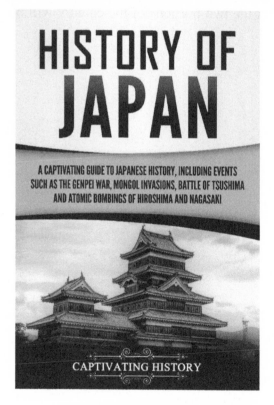

HISTORY OF
TAIWAN

A CAPTIVATING GUIDE TO TAIWANESE HISTORY AND THE RELATIONSHIP WITH THE PEOPLE'S REPUBLIC OF CHINA

CAPTIVATING HISTORY

References

Choy, B. (2012). *Korea: A History*. Tuttle Publishing Company.

Ho, J., Gamarra, E.R. (2016). *The Globally Important Agricultural Wisdom in the 15th Century Choson Korea*. The Academy of Korean Studies.

Jho, W. (2013). *Building Telecom Markets: Evolution of Governance in the Korean Mobile*. Springer Books.

Kim, J. (2012). *A History of Korea: From "Land of the Morning Calm" to States in Conflict*. Indiana State University Press.

Kim, M. (2014). *Law and Custom in Korea: Comparative Legal History*. Cambridge University Press.

Kim, Bumsheol "Socioeconomic Development in the Bronze Age". Retrieved from https://scholarspace.manoa.hawaii.edu/bitstream/10125/55550/07_A P_54.1kim.pdf

"Korean Confucianism". Retrieved from http://intl.ikorea.ac.kr/korean/UserFiles/UKS3_Korean_Confucianis m_eng.pdf

Lee, P. (ed.) (1983). *Anthology of Korean Literature: From the Earliest Era to the Nineteenth Century*. University of Hawaii Press.

Mintz, Gordon (ed.), Ra Hung Ha (trans) (2006). *Samguk Yusa: The History of the Three Kingdoms*. Silk Pagoda.

"The Miracle with a Dark Side". Retrieved from https://www.piie.com/publications/chapters_preview/341/3iie3373.pdf "The Miracle with a Dark Side," 1980 From Reforming Korea.

Park, E. B., Jackson, B. (trans) (2017). *Letters from Korea,* Vol. 2. Cum Libro.

Pulsik, K. Shutz, E. (ed.) (2011). *The Koguryo Annals of the Samguk Sagi*. Academy of Korean Studies.

Rawski, E. S. (2015). *Modern China and Northeast Asia: Cross-Border Perspectives*. Cambridge University Press.

Shin, J. S. (2014) *A Brief History of Korea*, Vol. 1: "The Spirit of Korean Cultural Roots" (2005). Ewa Women's University Press.

Tang, L, Winkler, Dietmar (ed) (2017). *Hidden Treasures and Intercultural Encounters*.

Tennant, R. (2012). *History of Korea*. Routledge.

Made in the USA
Coppell, TX
30 November 2020

42476792R00073

HISTORY OF KOREA

The Korean Peninsula today is divided into two, but there was a time when this peninsula was divided into many states. Over the course of time, and besieged by expansive transient dynasties outside of this modest piece of land, many clans and tribes overran their lands. Of all those malicious and greedy potential overlords, none managed to prevail. The soil is rich with the blood of the people who made Korea happen, and it is the Korean people who rose victorious among the maelstrom of dead empires led by hated tyrants and wars fought by people in lands far beyond their own. The Koreans are survivors, known for their persistence and courage.

As Korea had long been seen as a gateway to other countries and the Yellow Sea, it was harassed for years by larger countries who were either on their way to somewhere else, like China, or who wanted a springboard to control the trade and colonization of the archipelagoes, smaller countries, and islands around the Pacific Ocean. The Western countries had interests in Korea, too, in order to curtail the full control of the Pacific to only one country, as well as to open Korea up to trade. As a result of these competing forces, Korea isolated itself during the latter half of the 19th century. In 1910, Japan annexed Korea and ruled it with an iron fist, even to the point of assimilating the unique culture of Korea into its own culture. In other words, they wanted to make it "disappear." The Koreans, however, fought long and hard to preserve their individuality as a nation. They eschewed control by other forces, even friendly ones, in order to preserve their unique cultural and political identity.

About Captivating History

A lot of history books just contain dry facts that will eventually bore the reader. That's why Captivating History was created. Now you can enjoy history books that will mesmerize you. But be careful though, hours can fly by, and before you know it; you're up reading way past bedtime.

Make sure to follow us on Twitter, Facebook and Youtube by searching for Captivating History.

ISBN 9781647483753

9 781647 483753

90000